Language Lessons for a Living Education

First printing: August 2018
Third printing: August 2019

Copyright © 2018 by Kristen Pratt. All rights reserved. No part of this book may be used or reproduced in any manner whatsoever without written permission of the publisher, except in the case of brief quotations in articles and reviews. For information write:

Master Books®, P.O. Box 726, Green Forest, AR 72638

Master Books® is a division of the New Leaf Publishing Group, Inc.

ISBN: 978-1-68344-137-3
ISBN: 978-1-61458-678-4 (digital)

Unless otherwise noted, Scripture quotations taken from the New American Standard Bible® (NASB). Copyright © 1960, 1962, 1963, 1968, 1971, 1972, 1973, 1975, 1977, 1995 by The Lockman Foundation. Used by permission. www.Lockman.org.

Printed in the United States of America

Please visit our website for other great titles: www.masterbooks.com.

For information regarding author interviews, please contact the publicity department at (870) 438-5288.

Permission is granted for copies of reproducible pages from this text to be made for use within your own homeschooling family activities. Material may not be posted online, distributed digitally, or made available as a download. Permission for any other use of the material must be requested prior to use by email to the publisher at info@nlpg.com.

All images shutterstock.com or istockphotos.com unless indicated.

Page 29 from *The 10 Minute Bible Journey*, courtesy of Master Books; Page 101 Goodsalt.com
Page 133 Public Domain; Page 173 from *Giants Legends and Lore of Goliaths*, courtesy of Master Books;
Page 207 Public Domain; Page 297 courtesy of Master Books;

Scope and Sequence

Using This Course 4
Daily Schedule 13
Lesson 1: Story, Alphabet Review, Sentence Review, Reading, Short A, E Words................. 21
Lesson 2: Picture Study, Noun Review, Calendar, Reading, Short I, O, U Words.................. 29
Lesson 3: Story, Proper Nouns, Pronouns, Calendar, Reading, Long A Words...................... 37
Lesson 4: Poem, Plural Nouns, Calendar, Reading, Long E Words.. 45
Lesson 5: Story, Plural Nouns, Sentence Types, Reading, Long I Words............................... 53
Lesson 6: Picture Study, Plural Nouns, Commas, Reading, Long O Words........................... 61
Lesson 7: Story, Plural Nouns, Abbreviations, Reading, Long U Words................................ 69
Lesson 8: Psalm, Possessive Nouns, Sentences, Reading, Sight Words.................................. 77
Lesson 9: Reading, 1st Quarter Review, Reading, 1st Quarter Spelling Review..................... 85
Lesson 10: Story, Action Verbs, Sentence Combining, Reading, -ed, -ing Words.................. 93
Lesson 11: Picture Study, State of Being Verbs, Compound Words, Reading, /oy/, /oi/ Words 101
Lesson 12: Story, Adjectives, Contractions, Reading, /ar/, /or/, /er/, /ir/, /ur/ Words 109
Lesson 13: Poem, Adverbs, Quotation Marks, Reading, Plural -s, -es Words........................ 117
Lesson 14: Story, Prepositions, Titles, Reading, Plural f to v, y to i Words........................... 125
Lesson 15: Picture Study, Homophones, Dictionary Guide Words, Reading, Irregular Plural Words...... 133
Lesson 16: Story, Homophones, Sentences Review, Reading, Compound Words................. 141
Lesson 17: Psalm, Articles, Writing a Paragraph, Reading, Contractions 147
Lesson 18: Story, 2nd Quarter Review, Reading, 2nd Quarter Spelling Review 155
Lesson 19: Story, Verbs, Combining Sentences, Reading, -air, -are, -oar, -ore, -ure Words...... 165
Lesson 20: Picture Study, Helping Verbs, Synonyms, Antonyms, Thesaurus, Reading,
    pl, pr, sh, th Words 173
Lesson 21: Story, Verb Usage, Homonyms, Homophones, Reading, ck, ct, ft, ld, mp, nd Words............. 181
Lesson 22: Poem, Verb Usage, Prefix un-, re-, Reading, Homophones.................................. 189
Lesson 23: Story, Word Usage, Prefix in-, im-, dis-, pre-, tele-, Reading, Homonyms........... 197
Lesson 24: Picture Study, Word Usage, Suffix -ed, -ing, Root Words, Reading,
    Prefix dis-, im-, in-, re-, un- Words 207
Lesson 25: Story, Word Usage, Simile, Reading, Suffix -est, -ied, -less, -ly, -y Words 215
Lesson 26: Psalm, Comparison, Writing a Paragraph, Reading, Roots bio, graph, phon, scope Words ... 223
Lesson 27: Story, 3rd Quarter Review, Reading, 3rd Quarter Spelling Review..................... 231
Lesson 28: Story, Noun Review, Sentence Review, Reading, -ng, -nk, -nt, -pt, -sk, -st Words................ 239
Lesson 29: Picture Study, Plural Nouns Review, Sentence Review, Reading, -ch, -tch Words................ 247
Lesson 30: Story, Preposition Review, Quotation Marks, Reading, spr, shr, str, squ, scr, spl, thr Words .. 255
Lesson 31: Poem, Review, Reading, f, gh, ph Words 263
Lesson 32: Story, Verb Review, Similes, Reading, Soft and Hard g Words 271
Lesson 33: Picture Study, Word Usage Review, Reading, Silent Letter Words 279
Lesson 34: Story, Adjectives/Adverbs Review, Paragraph Review, Reading, Double Consonant Words .. 287
Lesson 35: Psalm, Word Usage Review, 4th Quarter Review, Reading, Ordinal Number Words 295
Lesson 36: Story, 4th Quarter Review, Thank You Letter, Reading, 4th Quarter Spelling Review 305
Teacher Aids.. 315

Using This Course

Features: The suggested weekly schedule enclosed has easy-to-manage lessons that guide the reading, worksheets, and all assessments. The pages of this guide are perforated and three-hole punched so materials are easy to tear out, hand out, grade, and store. Teachers are encouraged to adjust the schedule and materials needed in order to best work within their unique educational program.

Lesson Scheduling: Students are instructed to read the pages in their book and then complete the corresponding section provided by the teacher. Assessments that may include worksheets, activities, and reviews are given at regular intervals with space to record each grade. Space is provided on the weekly schedule for assignment dates, and flexibility in scheduling is encouraged. Teachers may adapt the scheduled days per each unique student situation. As the student completes each assignment, this can be marked with an "X" in the box.

🕐	Approximately 20 to 30 minutes per lesson, five days a week
🔑	Includes answer keys for worksheets
📝	Worksheets
📄	Reviews are included to help reinforce learning and provide assessment opportunities
🔄	Designed for grade 3 in a one-year course

Course Objectives: Students completing this course will:

- Master state of being verbs, action verbs, and possessive nouns
- Review sentences, singular and plural nouns, adjectives and adverbs
- Identify abbreviations, proper use of punctuation marks, spelling, root words, compound words, and suffixes
- Create their own dictionary with words learned through the course
- Learn to create good paragraphs based on structure and comprehension
- Develop skills in using the dictionary and a thesaurus for spelling and vocabulary-building
- Explore the Scripture, parts of letter writing, copywork, and more!

Course Description

Language Lessons for a Living Education 3 is a Charlotte Mason–flavored approach to elementary language arts. Enjoy an engaging and effective language arts program for your elementary student. Students will move beyond pages of text and memorization to make real-world connections. This exciting new series will help guide your young learner toward mastery of reading, grammar, and vocabulary, as well as the mechanics of communication and writing. Utilizing phonics, observation, and reading comprehension through poems, stories, and real books as the foundation, your student will begin to write paragraphs.

The course is a story-based approach, using Charlotte Mason ideas for the modern homeschool student with character-building themes. Each quarter has five stories, two picture studies (one of which is biblically-based), and two poems (one of which is a Psalm). Using the spelling words and the Dictionary Worksheets, the student will create their very own dictionary as they move week by week through the material. This course incorporates picture study, memorization, grammar and punctuation, spelling and vocabulary, observation, and application through creating their own stories through pictures, sentences, paragraphs, poems, psalms, and letters. This course also develops reading skills and gently develops narration skills. Writing stamina is built up gradually. By the end of the course, students should be able to comfortably write a four to five sentence paragraph.

Required Course Materials: This course has an integrated reading component that uses *101 Favorite Stories from the Bible*, also available from Master Books.

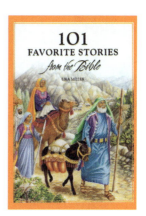

A Note from the Author

This course was written with inspiration from classic educators like Charlotte Mason and Emma Serl. It was also inspired by homeschool educators like David Marks, Angela O'Dell, Katherine Loop, and my colleagues, Craig Froman and Laura Welch. If you could put these people in a room, you would find they all have different thoughts on how to educate a child, yet they have all taught me something that has gone into this series. I have tried to take the effective principles from long ago and update them for a modern world with the hope of inspiring a new generation to communicate their faith, and the gospel, to their generation.

A special thanks goes to Becki Dudley who helped write the stories in this level. Thank you to Craig Froman who created the Make Your Own Dictionary concept. Also, thanks to Diana Bogardus for creating the cover, setting the tone and beautiful feel of this course. Thank you to Jennifer Bauer for the hours of design work to marry function with beauty. Thank you to Laura Welch and the proofers for their insights and wisdom.

I am indebted to the Moms of Masterbooks who give us valuable feedback on how to improve our curriculum to meet their needs. We do this for them. It is our goal to come alongside them and provide the tools they need to bring up a godly generation, known by the Lord. When the days feel long, I think of the impact our work is having on homeschooled children, and my strength is renewed. Thank you for allowing us to partner with you in the education of your children.

Of course, my children have taught me, for many years, principles of education that have surprised and inspired me. I have often marveled that nine children can grow up in the same home and be so different from each other. We truly are wonderfully and fearfully made. I have learned that curriculum needs to be flexible to meet the needs of the unique individuals God has entrusted to our care.

May God bless and keep you, and give you wisdom and strength, as you homeschool your children in the nurture and admonition of the Lord.

Blessings,

Kristen Pratt

About this Course

- Children enjoy patterns. They like to have rhythms in life that they can count on. This course is set up in a pattern that students and teachers alike can rely on.

The first day of the weekly schedule is a special feature. Every other week starts with a short story. The weeks in between alternate between picture studies and reading poetry or a psalm. (Each quarter follows this pattern.) A light lesson follows.

The second and third days of the week cover writing topics such as grammar and punctuation. They are the tools put into the hands of the student to use when they write.

On the fourth day of the week, students read from *101 Favorite Stories from the Bible* by Ura Miller, published by Master Books. These stories may be read out loud by the teacher, student, or both. We encourage students to read as much as possible to strengthen their skills and stamina. There are three narration prompts following each reading. Next, the student will write out a Scripture verse for copy work. The student and teacher should memorize this Scripture verse together. Each story has a beautiful illustration that the student will sketch.

The fifth day is when the student focuses on spelling and vocabulary, building a dictionary of words they can use in their writing.

- There are patterns within the lessons themselves. Students are given a variety of activities that repeat themselves every so often. This creates familiarity without overdoing repetition.

Students' reading abilities, hand-eye coordination, and stamina vary widely at this age. We have started the course gently, gradually increasing the amounts of reading and writing. Feel free to adjust the pace according to the needs of your student. We have also given varied types of material in the back of the book to aid in the extra practice of key concepts.

There is review built into the course. You will find some topics repeated regularly. Others are repeated in the last quarter when the student will review most of the material they have learned. This is vital at this level since so many of the topics are fairly new to the student. It is the perfect opportunity to shore up any areas the student needs to work on.

We hope you enjoy using this course with your student. It is designed to foster a partnership between student and teacher, with the student gradually taking a lead role. Allowing the student's growing abilities, stamina, and interests to set the pace will strengthen the student's confidence. This confidence is the key that will help unlock communication success.

Teaching Helps

Stories, Poems, Psalms

The stories, poems, and psalms were designed for the teacher and student to read together. This gives reading practice and experience within the context of a short story or passage. This method fosters a partnership between the teacher and the student. It allows the teacher to see where the student excels and where the student needs some extra instruction. It also gives the student a safe place to practice their developing reading skills.

The sentences we suggest for the student to read are highlighted. The number, length, and complexity of the suggested sentences are gradually increased. These serve as suggestions only. The ability and stamina of the student should guide the pace. Some students will need a slower pace, while other students may want to read more than the suggested sentences.

The student should read as much of the story, poem, or psalm as possible. The teacher should help the student sound out difficult words and gently take over the reading if the student tires or is struggling. The goal is to build reading skills and stamina slowly, through practice. Care should be taken to stay light-hearted and encouraging. Students this age can become discouraged if reading doesn't come easily and quickly. Extra encouragement, patience, and instruction may be needed to smooth over the bumps and to keep the student engaged in the process.

If a student is struggling to read, sometimes their short-term memory needs to be developed. Reading is memory intensive. The student must remember the start of a word while sounding out the end. They must also remember what they read in the first part of the sentence as they finish reading the end of the sentence. Then they must remember the sequence of events within the story. There is a lot to remember, especially when they are concentrating on words they do not know. You can work on increasing short-term memory through memory games. You will find some in the back of the book.

The NASB is used for the psalms and all Scripture passages (unless otherwise noted) in this book, but you may use the version you prefer.

Independent Reading

Work with the student to pick a book for the student to read independently over the course of the week. Care should be taken to select a book within the student's reading ability.

Depending on the reading ability of the student, the book may be read orally, with the help of the teacher. Students may also choose to read the book independently, asking for help only when they come to a word they cannot read or do not understand.

You will find in the back of the book a list of reading book suggestions and a place to record the books the student has read or plans to read.

Oral Narration

Oral narration (or telling back) helps a student develop listening skills and reading comprehension. These questions will help a student connect with the story and improve basic narration skills.

Oral narration is a skill that needs to be developed. Oral narration teaches the student to pay attention to the story and to think about what is happening. It fosters memory recall, which helps develop reading skills. The questions are meant to gently lead a student to the goal of being able to tell back a story on their own, with no prompts. Students will vary greatly in their ability to narrate back to the teacher a whole story. We suggest a slow approach, testing a student now and then to see if they can do it without the prompts.

Memorization

Throughout the course, there are opportunities to memorize short passages of Scripture, poems, etc. The teacher should participate with the student and memorize them, too. Students this age are naturally good at memorizing, but they may need some encouragement. Modeling and working together is the best way to encourage this skill.

The students will be memorizing Philippians 4:4–9 and Colossians 3:12–15, two verses at a time. Two weeks are given to learn each set of verses. The teacher should memorize the verses with the student. The class in the story earns a prize once they have recited the whole passage. It would be fun and rewarding (but optional) for you to provide a small prize for your student after they have memorized all the verses.

Writing a Paragraph

Students will be introduced to writing a paragraph. Each time a student is asked to write a paragraph, they are provided with a checklist to remind them of the structure of a paragraph. We have also provided this checklist in the back of the book. They are given the chance to write a paragraph with a variety of prompts to appeal to many types of students. For example, they are asked to write about things they like and are personal to them but sometimes the prompt is a picture.

Students may struggle to write a cohesive paragraph, but with practice, they will improve. It is good to remind students about using proper punctuation. If they make a mistake, have them correct it but encourage them about what a great job they did. There are different schools of thought regarding whether to correct spelling mistakes. Some do not want the student to learn to spell words the wrong way by having what they wrote imprinted. Others do not want to discourage the student's writing by having the student fix spelling mistakes. Students vary widely in their ability and personality. I would encourage approaching it on a case-by-case basis. You know your student best!

If the student struggles to write a paragraph, you can shorten the assignment to the topic sentence, detail sentence, and a closing sentence. If the struggle is stamina, you may write part of the paragraph for the student. You may also want to have the struggling student organize their thoughts by reciting what they want to say to you before they start to write. You can also encourage the student by asking them questions to lead them through the process. For example, you could say, "Ok, you have a great topic sentence about your cat. What are some things you want to tell about your cat?"

Some students will not master writing a paragraph at this level. Some students will master it the first time they write one. The goal is for the student to improve over the school year, regardless of their ability level. Even writers who are slower to learn this skill can learn to love writing through lots of gentle encouragement.

Picture Sketching

Whether a student is naturally gifted at drawing or not, this activity develops hand-eye coordination, observation skills, and overall drawing abilities. Each Bible story has a beautiful image for the student to copy. Some students will be very detailed in their sketches while other students will draw the bare minimum. We encourage teachers to allow students to start where their abilities are. Progress is the goal, not perfection. We want students to enjoy the process. If drawing is difficult for the student, we recommend picking out one element of the picture for the student to draw. The student may want to use colored pencils to bring their sketches to life. Be sure to lavish the student's attempts with praise and encouragement.

Spelling & Vocabulary

There are various types of activities to foster experience with words. The student should study how to spell the words and use them as often as possible.

Some students will struggle more than others with spelling. We have provided resources in the back of the book that include:

- A list of the spelling words organized by lesson for testing, practice, and Make Your Own Dictionary
- A place to keep a list of words to work on
- Extra spelling activities and games

Pronunciations can vary by region. Students may be asked to complete activities based on the vowel sound in a word. Please adjust any such assignments or lessons according to the pronunciation used by your family.

Handwriting

While this is not a formal handwriting course, each time a student writes, it is an opportunity to practice handwriting. It is good to remind students to write neatly, using their best penmanship. Copywork at the back of the book may be used for more handwriting practice. We also suggest using Scripture as copywork for handwriting practice.

Create Your Own Dictionary!

With the teacher's help, the student will use the spelling words and the Dictionary Worksheets to create their very own dictionary.

The teacher will need to make copies of the Create Your Own Dictionary! sheets in the back of the book as needed. They are also available for download on our website. If the student struggles to add all the words to their dictionary, the teacher may let them pick fewer words. Let the student's ability and stamina be the guide.

The student will write out the word, draw a picture that shows each word, and then finish with a simple definition.

This is a good opportunity to introduce a children's dictionary to the student. The teacher should demonstrate how to look up words in a dictionary and use it to complete the definitions. The student may use a simple definition rather than copy directly from the dictionary.

The student is encouraged to remove the dictionary pages and continue to add words to it long after they have finished the course. The teacher may offer blank Create Your Own Dictionary! pages for this purpose.

For Fun!

"Just 4 Fun" activities provide extra thinking and problem solving practice. They are meant to be fun. If a student has difficulty solving an activity, offer hints and encouragement. If the student is unable to find the solution, walk him or her through the process of how to solve the problem. Be sure to provide the answer.

Review

The fourth quarter reviews lessons the student has learned in the first three quarters. This is crucial for students to master the material. The lesson length is longer since the student is familiar with the material. If the student does not have the stamina to complete the longer lessons, there are several options. The teacher may read the work to the student, letting the student do the written portion. The teacher may allow the student to complete some of the problems orally. The teacher may also spread the work over several days, as needed.

In addition to the fourth quarter review, there are Quarterly Reviews at the end of each quarter. See Assessments on the next page.

Teacher Aids

In the back of the book, you will find a section of Teacher Aids. These aids include assessments, extra practice pages, study sheets, fun games, and more. We encourage you to look through the tools provided to use with your students. They provide opportunities for enrichment and fun as your student learns how to communicate more effectively.

Assessments

Two types of assessments are provided.

We have provided Quarterly Reviews within the curriculum at the end of each quarter. Each quarter has two Reviews covering punctuation, grammar, and writing. There is also a spelling Review. The three Reviews provided each quarter may be used as quizzes or tests for grading purposes. At this level, we recommend using an open book approach for Quarterly Reviews. Students should have access to the Study Sheets in the back of the book when completing Reviews.

We have also provided an Assessment form in the back of the book that may be used for grading purposes. It tracks mastery of concepts taught throughout the course.

First Semester Suggested Daily Schedule

Date	Day	Assignment	Due Date	✓	Grade
		First Semester-First Quarter			
Week 1	Day 1	Read Story • Page 21 Complete Lesson 1 Exercise 1 • Page 22			
	Day 2	Complete Lesson 1 Exercise 2 • Pages 23-24			
	Day 3	Complete Lesson 1 Exercise 3 • Page 25			
	Day 4	Complete Lesson 1 Exercise 4 • Page 26			
	Day 5	Complete Lesson 1 Exercise 5 • Pages 27-28			
Week 2	Day 6	Picture Study • Page 29 Complete Lesson 2 Exercise 1 • Page 30			
	Day 7	Complete Lesson 2 Exercise 2 • Page 31			
	Day 8	Complete Lesson 2 Exercise 3 • Pages 32-33			
	Day 9	Complete Lesson 2 Exercise 4 • Page 34			
	Day 10	Complete Lesson 2 Exercise 5 • Pages 35-36			
Week 3	Day 11	Read Story • Page 37 Complete Lesson 3 Exercise 1 • Page 38			
	Day 12	Complete Lesson 3 Exercise 2 • Pages 39-40			
	Day 13	Complete Lesson 3 Exercise 3 • Page 41			
	Day 14	Complete Lesson 3 Exercise 4 • Page 42			
	Day 15	Complete Lesson 3 Exercise 5 • Pages 43-44			
Week 4	Day 16	Read Poem • Page 45 Complete Lesson 4 Exercise 1 • Page 46			
	Day 17	Complete Lesson 4 Exercise 2 • Page 47			
	Day 18	Complete Lesson 4 Exercise 3 • Pages 48-49			
	Day 19	Complete Lesson 4 Exercise 4 • Page 50			
	Day 20	Complete Lesson 4 Exercise 5 • Pages 51-52			
Week 5	Day 21	Read Story • Page 53 Complete Lesson 5 Exercise 1 • Page 54			
	Day 22	Complete Lesson 5 Exercise 2 • Page 55			
	Day 23	Complete Lesson 5 Exercise 3 • Pages 56-57			
	Day 24	Complete Lesson 5 Exercise 4 • Page 58			
	Day 25	Complete Lesson 5 Exercise 5 • Pages 59-60			
Week 6	Day 26	Picture Study • Page 61 Complete Lesson 6 Exercise 1 • Page 62			
	Day 27	Complete Lesson 6 Exercise 2 • Page 63			
	Day 28	Complete Lesson 6 Exercise 3 • Pages 64-65			
	Day 29	Complete Lesson 6 Exercise 4 • Page 66			
	Day 30	Complete Lesson 6 Exercise 5 • Pages 67-69			

Language Level 3 — Daily Schedule

Date	Day	Assignment	Due Date	✓	Grade
Week 7	Day 31	Read Story • Page 69 Complete Lesson 7 Exercise 1 • Page 70			
	Day 32	Complete Lesson 7 Exercise 2 • Pages 71-72			
	Day 33	Complete Lesson 7 Exercise 3 • Pages 73-74			
	Day 34	Complete Lesson 7 Exercise 4 • Page 75			
	Day 35	Complete Lesson 7 Exercise 5 • Pags 76			
Week 8	Day 36	Read Psalm 20 • Page 77 Complete Lesson 8 Exercise 1 • Page 78			
	Day 37	Complete Lesson 8 Exercise 2 • Pages 79-80			
	Day 38	Complete Lesson 8 Exercise 3 • Pages 81-82			
	Day 39	Complete Lesson 8 Exercise 4 • Page 83			
	Day 40	Complete Lesson 8 Exercise 5 • Page 84			
Week 9	Day 41	Read Story • Page 85 Complete Lesson 9 Exercise 1 • Page 86			
	Day 42	Do Lesson 9 Exercise 2 **(Quarter 1 Review)** • Pages 87-88			
	Day 43	Do Lesson 9 Exercise 3 **(Quarter 1 Review)** • Pages 89-90			
	Day 44	Complete Lesson 9 Exercise 4 • Page 91			
	Day 45	Complete Lesson 9 Exercise 5 • Page 92			
		First Semester-Second Quarter			
Week 1	Day 46	Read Story • Page 93 Complete Lesson 10 Exercise 1 • Page 94			
	Day 47	Complete Lesson 10 Exercise 2 • Pages 95-96			
	Day 48	Complete Lesson 10 Exercise 3 • Pages 97-98			
	Day 49	Complete Lesson 10 Exercise 4 • Page 99			
	Day 50	Complete Lesson 10 Exercise 5 • Page 100			
Week 2	Day 51	Picture Study • Page 101 Complete Lesson 11 Exercise 1 • Page 102			
	Day 52	Complete Lesson 11 Exercise 2 • Pages 103-104			
	Day 53	Complete Lesson 11 Exercise 3 • Pages 105-106			
	Day 54	Complete Lesson 11 Exercise 4 • Page 107			
	Day 55	Complete Lesson 11 Exercise 5 • Page 108			
Week 3	Day 56	Read Story • Page 109 Complete Lesson 12 Exercise 1 • Page 110			
	Day 57	Complete Lesson 12 Exercise 2 • Pages 111-112			
	Day 58	Complete Lesson 12 Exercise 3 • Pages 113-114			
	Day 59	Complete Lesson 12 Exercise 4 • Page 115			
	Day 60	Complete Lesson 12 Exercise 5 • Page 116			
Week 4	Day 61	Read Poem • Page 117 Complete Lesson 13 Exercise 1 • Page 118			
	Day 62	Complete Lesson 13 Exercise 2 • Pages 119-120			
	Day 63	Complete Lesson 13 Exercise 3 • Pages 121-122			
	Day 64	Complete Lesson 13 Exercise 4 • Page 123			
	Day 65	Complete Lesson 13 Exercise 5 • Page 124			

Date	Day	Assignment	Due Date	✓	Grade
Week 5	Day 66	Read Story • Page 125 Complete Lesson 14 Exercise 1 • Page 126			
	Day 67	Complete Lesson 14 Exercise 2 • Pages 127-128			
	Day 68	Complete Lesson 14 Exercise 3 • Pages 129-130			
	Day 69	Complete Lesson 14 Exercise 4 • Page 131			
	Day 70	Complete Lesson 14 Exercise 5 • Page 132			
Week 6	Day 71	Picture Study • Page 133 Complete Lesson 15 Exercise 1 • Page 134			
	Day 72	Complete Lesson 15 Exercise 2 • Page 135-136			
	Day 73	Complete Lesson 15 Exercise 3 • Pages 137-138			
	Day 74	Complete Lesson 15 Exercise 4 • Page 139			
	Day 75	Complete Lesson 15 Exercise 5 • Page 140			
Week 7	Day 76	Read Story • Page 141 Complete Lesson 16 Exercise 1 • Page 142			
	Day 77	Complete Lesson 16 Exercise 2 • Page 143			
	Day 78	Complete Lesson 16 Exercise 3 • Page 144			
	Day 79	Complete Lesson 16 Exercise 4 • Page 145			
	Day 80	Complete Lesson 16 Exercise 5 • Page 146			
Week 8	Day 81	Read Psalm 23 • Page 147 Complete Lesson 17 Exercise 1 • Page 148			
	Day 82	Complete Lesson 17 Exercise 2 • Pages 149-150			
	Day 83	Complete Lesson 17 Exercise 3 • Pages 151-152			
	Day 84	Complete Lesson 17 Exercise 4 • Page 153			
	Day 85	Complete Lesson 17 Exercise 5 • Page 154			
Week 9	Day 86	Read Story • Page 155 Complete Lesson 18 Exercise 1 • Page 156			
	Day 87	Do Lesson 18 Exercise 2 (**Quarter 2 Review**) • Pages 157-159			
	Day 88	Do Lesson 18 Exercise 3 (**Quarter 2 Review**) • Pages 160-162			
	Day 89	Complete Lesson 18 Exercise 4 • Page 163			
	Day 90	Complete Lesson 18 Exercise 5 • Page 164			
		Mid-Term Grade			

Second Semester Suggested Daily Schedule

Date	Day	Assignment	Due Date	✓	Grade
		Second Semester-Third Quarter			
Week 1	Day 91	Read Story • Page 165 Complete Lesson 19 Exercise 1 • Page 166			
	Day 92	Complete Lesson 19 Exercise 2 • Pages 167-168			
	Day 93	Complete Lesson 19 Exercise 3 • Pages 169-170			
	Day 94	Complete Lesson 19 Exercise 4 • Page 171			
	Day 95	Complete Lesson 19 Exercise 5 • Page 172			
Week 2	Day 96	Picture Study • Page 173 Complete Lesson 20 Exercise 1 • Page 174			
	Day 97	Complete Lesson 20 Exercise 2 • Pages 175-176			
	Day 98	Complete Lesson 20 Exercise 3 • Pages 177-178			
	Day 99	Complete Lesson 20 Exercise 4 • Page 179			
	Day 100	Complete Lesson 20 Exercise 5 • Page 180			
Week 3	Day 101	Read Story • Page 181 Complete Lesson 21 Exercise 1 • Page 182			
	Day 102	Complete Lesson 21 Exercise 2 • Pages 183-184			
	Day 103	Complete Lesson 21 Exercise 3 • Pages 185-186			
	Day 104	Complete Lesson 21 Exercise 4 • Page 187			
	Day 105	Complete Lesson 21 Exercise 5 • Page188			
Week 4	Day 106	Read Poem • Page 189 Complete Lesson 22 Exercise 1 • Page 190			
	Day 107	Complete Lesson 22 Exercise 2 • Pages 191-192			
	Day 108	Complete Lesson 22 Exercise 3 • Pages 193-194			
	Day 109	Complete Lesson 22 Exercise 4 • Page 195			
	Day 110	Complete Lesson 22 Exercise 5 • Page 196			
Week 5	Day 111	Read Story • Page 197 Complete Lesson 23 Exercise 1 • Pages 198-199			
	Day 112	Complete Lesson 23 Exercise 2 • Pages 200-202			
	Day 113	Complete Lesson 23 Exercise 3 • Pages 203-204			
	Day 114	Complete Lesson 23 Exercise 4 • Page 205			
	Day 115	Complete Lesson 23 Exercise 5 • Page 206			
Week 6	Day 116	Picture Study • Page 207 Complete Lesson 24 Exercise 1 • Page 208			
	Day 117	Complete Lesson 24 Exercise 2 • Page 209			
	Day 118	Complete Lesson 24 Exercise 3 • Pages 210-211			
	Day 119	Complete Lesson 24 Exercise 4 • Page 212			
	Day 120	Complete Lesson 24 Exercise 5 • Pages 213-214			

Date	Day	Assignment	Due Date	✓	Grade
Week 7	Day 121	Read Story • Page 215 Complete Lesson 25 Exercise 1 • Page 216			
	Day 122	Complete Lesson 25 Exercise 2 • Pages 217-218			
	Day 123	Complete Lesson 25 Exercise 3 • Pages 219-220			
	Day 124	Complete Lesson 25 Exercise 4 • Page 221			
	Day 125	Complete Lesson 25 Exercise 5 • Page 222			
Week 8	Day 126	Read Psalm 47 • Page 223 Complete Lesson 26 Exercise 1 • Page 224			
	Day 127	Complete Lesson 26 Exercise 2 • Pages 225-226			
	Day 128	Complete Lesson 26 Exercise 3 • Pages 227-228			
	Day 129	Complete Lesson 26 Exercise 4 • Page 229			
	Day 130	Complete Lesson 26 Exercise 5 • Page 230			
Week 9	Day 131	Read Story • Page 231 Complete Lesson 27 Exercise 1 • Page 232			
	Day 132	Do Lesson 27 Exercise 2 **(Quarter 3 Review)** • Pages 233-234			
	Day 133	Do Lesson 27 Exercise 3 **(Quarter 3 Review)** • Pages 235-236			
	Day 134	Complete Lesson 27 Exercise 4 • Page 237			
	Day 135	Complete Lesson 27 Exercise 5 • Page 238			
Second Semester-Fourth Quarter					
Week 1	Day 136	Read Story • Page 239 Complete Lesson 28 Exercise 1 • Page 240			
	Day 137	Complete Lesson 28 Exercise 2 • Pages 241-242			
	Day 138	Complete Lesson 28 Exercise 3 • Pages 243-244			
	Day 139	Complete Lesson 28 Exercise 4 • Page 245			
	Day 140	Complete Lesson 28 Exercise 5 • Page 246			
Week 2	Day 141	Picture Study • Page 247 Complete Lesson 29 Exercise 1 • Page 248			
	Day 142	Complete Lesson 29 Exercise 2 • Pages 249-250			
	Day 143	Complete Lesson 29 Exercise 3 • Pages 251-252			
	Day 144	Complete Lesson 29 Exercise 4 • Page 253			
	Day 145	Complete Lesson 29 Exercise 5 • Page 254			
Week 3	Day 146	Read Story • Page 255 Complete Lesson 30 Exercise 1 • Page 256			
	Day 147	Complete Lesson 30 Exercise 2 • Pages 257-258			
	Day 148	Complete Lesson 30 Exercise 3 • Page 259			
	Day 149	Complete Lesson 30 Exercise 4 • Page 260			
	Day 150	Complete Lesson 30 Exercise 5 • Pages 261-262			
Week 4	Day 151	Read Poem • Page 263 Complete Lesson 31 Exercise 1 • Page 264			
	Day 152	Complete Lesson 31 Exercise 2 • Pages 265-266			
	Day 153	Complete Lesson 31 Exercise 3 • Pages 267-268			
	Day 154	Complete Lesson 31 Exercise 4 • Page 269			
	Day 155	Complete Lesson 31 Exercise 5 • Page 270			

Date	Day	Assignment	Due Date	✓	Grade
Week 5	Day 156	Read Story • Page 271 Complete Lesson 32 Exercise 1 • Page 272			
	Day 157	Complete Lesson 32 Exercise 2 • Pages 273-275			
	Day 158	Complete Lesson 32 Exercise 3 • Page 276			
	Day 159	Complete Lesson 32 Exercise 4 • Page 277			
	Day 160	Complete Lesson 32 Exercise 5 • Page 278			
Week 6	Day 161	Picture Study • Page 279 Complete Lesson 33 Exercise 1 • Page 280			
	Day 162	Complete Lesson 33 Exercise 2 • Pages 281-282			
	Day 163	Complete Lesson 33 Exercise 3 • Pages 283-284			
	Day 164	Complete Lesson 33 Exercise 4 • Page 285			
	Day 165	Complete Lesson 33 Exercise 5 • Page 286			
Week 7	Day 166	Read Story • Page 287 Complete Lesson 34 Exercise 1 • Page 288			
	Day 167	Complete Lesson 34 Exercise 2 • Pages 289-290			
	Day 168	Complete Lesson 34 Exercise 3 • Pages 291-292			
	Day 169	Complete Lesson 34 Exercise 4 • Page 293			
	Day 170	Complete Lesson 34 Exercise 5 • Page 294			
Week 8	Day 171	Read Psalm 67 • Page 295 Complete Lesson 35 Exercise 1 • Page 296			
	Day 172	Complete Lesson 35 Exercise 2 • Pages 297-299			
	Day 173	Complete Lesson 35 Exercise 3 • Pages 300-302			
	Day 174	Complete Lesson 35 Exercise 4 • Page 303			
	Day 175	Complete Lesson 35 Exercise 5 • Page 304			
Week 9	Day 176	Read Story • Page 305 Complete Lesson 36 Exercise 1 • Pages 306-307			
	Day 177	Do Lesson 36 Exercise 2 **(Quarter 4 Review)** • Pages 308-310			
	Day 178	Do Lesson 36 Exercise 3 **(Quarter 4 Review)** • Pages 311-312			
	Day 179	Complete Lesson 36 Exercise 4 • Page 313			
	Day 180	Complete Lesson 36 Exercise 5 • Page 314			
		Final Grade			

Lesson 1

Move Up! Day

It was the start of a new school year. Micah and Claire were excited about Sunday school at their church. It was Move Up! Day, and they wondered who their teacher would be. The two friends found their new classroom and quickly took a seat. All the children were excited to see a special snack waiting for them! Before long, a friendly face popped into the class. It was Mr. Lopez! Micah, Claire, and the other students looked at each other, wondering if Mr. Lopez was going to introduce the new teacher. He began, "I have a special announcement to make. I hope you aren't disappointed, but I am going to be your teacher again this year!" The students were surprised. Some of them giggled before the whole class clapped with joy. Mr. Lopez smiled, laughed, then thanked the class for their kindness.

Mr. Lopez started the lesson by explaining that God likes it when we celebrate and give thanks to Him. He talked about the different feasts and celebrations described in the Bible. Mr. Lopez explained that the spring feasts are Passover, Unleavened Bread, First Fruits, and Pentecost. He said the fall Feasts are Trumpets, The Day of Atonement, and Tabernacles. Micah was surprised there are so many! They all sounded so strange, but he was eager to learn more about them. Mr. Lopez said they would learn a lot more about these special celebrations in the future, but for now, they would celebrate Move Up! Day with donuts and cider!

- Please review Reading and Narration tips at the beginning of the book.

(1) How does this story start?

(2) Why did Mr. Lopez come into the class?

(3) What kind of celebrations did Mr. Lopez talk about?

(4) How does the story end?

Language Level 3 – Lesson 1

Name _____   Exercise 1   Day 1

The Alphabet

 **TEACHER NOTE** • There is an alphabet in the back of the book for students to review if needed.

Do you remember how to say your alphabet? Say it to your teacher.

Do you remember the vowels? Say them to your teacher.

Grouping

Draw a picture of something that goes with each group of items.

22 Language Level 3 – Lesson 1

Name_____ Exercise 2 Day 2

The Alphabet

Write your alphabet using colored pencils. Write the upper-case and the lower-case letters. Write the consonants with a blue pencil. Write the vowels with a red pencil.

(1) _____

(2) _____

(3) _____

(4) _____

(5) _____

(6) _____

(7) _____

(8) _____

(9) _____

(10) _____

(11) _____

(12) _____

(13) _____

(14) _____

(15) _____

(16) _____

(17) _____

(18) _____

(19) _____

(20) _____

(21) _____

(22) _____

(23) _____

(24) _____

(25) _____

(26) _____

Language Level 3 – Lesson 1

Exercise 2 — Day 2

All the letters!

There is a popular sentence that uses every letter in the alphabet:

The quick brown fox jumps over the lazy dog.

(1) Using the spaces below each letter, number them from 1-26 in order. For example, a = 1, z = 26. **Hint:** Sing your alphabet song while you do it!

T h e   q u i c k   b r o w n
___ ___ ___   ___ ___ ___ ___ ___   ___ ___ ___ ___ ___

f o x   j u m p s   o v e r
___ ___ ___   ___ ___ ___ ___ ___   ___ ___ ___ ___

t h e   l a z y   d o g.
___ ___ ___   ___ ___ ___ ___   ___ ___ ___

Note: The sentence uses several letters more than once.

(2) The sentence also has 6 letters that were used more than once. What are those letters?

_____, _____, _____, _____, _____, _____.

(3) What letter was used more than the others in the sentence? _____

Language Level 3 – Lesson 1

Capitalization and Punctuation

Do you remember what we use at the beginning of the first word when we write a sentence? Yes, a capital letter.

Do you remember what we end a sentence with? Yes, a punctuation mark.

Do you remember the three types of punctuation marks we use to end a sentence? We use a period, question mark, or an exclamation point.

Write the correct punctuation mark after each sentence.

(1) What are the feasts in the Bible____

(2) Mr. Lopez is our teacher____

(3) I can't wait to eat a donut____

Write a sentence that asks a question.

_____
_____

Did you start your sentence with a capital letter? Did you end it with a question mark? If not, be sure to fix it.

- See instructions for Independent Reading in the front of the book.
- Discuss with the student who an author is and where the name of the author can be found.

Name _____   Exercise 4   Day 4

 READING COMPREHENSION

 TEACHER NOTE
- Review Reading Tips in the beginning of the book. Students are to give oral answers to the questions in *101 Favorite Stories from the Bible*.

Read pages 10–11 with your teacher of *101 Favorite Stories from the Bible*.

Answer the questions on page 11.

Copy Hebrews 11:3, then memorize it with your teacher.

Copy the picture on page 11 and color it. Draw the whole picture or just choose one or two things from the picture. Copy the caption from page 11 below.

Language Level 3 – Lesson 1

Name_____   Exercise **5**   Day 5

 **Short -a and -e Sound Words**

We are going to work with words that make the short -a and -e sound.

Learn to spell these words:

> ask, basket, candy, check, damp,
> every, help, left, next, stand

Choose spelling words to fill in the blanks in the sentences.

(1) Micah needed _____ to reach the sweet _____.

(2) He will _____ if he can put the pretty flowers in the _____.

(3) Claire's shirt was _____ after she _____ it in the rain.

(4) Claire and Micah will _____ _____ to each other.

(5) Micah and Claire _____ _____ answer to make sure they are right.

Language Level 3 – Lesson 1

Exercise 5 — Day 5

Write a fun sentence using at least two of your spelling words. Be sure to start your sentence with a capital letter and end it with a punctuation mark.

_____
_____
_____

Write your spelling words on notecards. Write one word on each card. You may create right-brain flashcards with your words. (See page 346 for right-brain flashcard ideas.)

Optional Activities

• If student needs more practice, you may assign these additional activities.

Write your spelling words.

(1) _____   (6) _____

(2) _____   (7) _____

(3) _____   (8) _____

(4) _____   (9) _____

(5) _____   (10) _____

Ask your teacher to read each spelling word. Spell the word out loud to your teacher and use it in a sentence.

• See instructions for Dictionary in the back of the book.

 **PICTURE STUDY**

Lesson 2

Title: Moses & the Burning Bush

Artist: Robert Forest & Lucas Silveira

 **OBSERVATION SKILLS**

(1) Who is in the picture?

(2) What is happening in the picture?

(3) What colors are used in the picture?

(4) How does this picture make you feel? Why?

(used with permission of Dale Mason, *The 10 Minute Bible Journey*)

Language Level 3 – Lesson 2

29

Name _____   Exercise 1   Day 6

Sight Words

Read the following words to your teacher. After you read all the words, create sight word memory cards using index cards. Write on a separate card each word the teacher circled. Ask your teacher if you need to add any other words to the list.

- Circle all words the student must sound out, reads slowly, or needs help reading. Help the student create sight word memory cards as needed. Add to the list any other common words that the student has difficulty reading.
- If student tires, this activity may be spread out over several days, using the breaks between as needed.

about	clean	drink	full	hot
better	cut	eight	got	hurt
bring	done	fall	grow	if
carry	draw	far	hold	keep
laugh	myself	pick	six	today
light	never	seven	small	together
long	only	shall	start	try
much	own	show	ten	warm

(Dolch words: The list was prepared in 1936 by Edward William Dolch and was originally published in his book *Problems in Reading* in 1948.)

Name _____ Exercise 2 Day 7

Nouns

A common *noun* is a person, place, or thing.

A *proper noun* names a person, place, or thing.
A proper noun begins with a capital letter.

Write the first and last name of a parent or relative. Remember to use a capital letter for the first letter of both the first and last name.

W Baby Stoll

Write a sentence using a proper noun that names a place.

I Love Boby.

Did you start your sentence with a capital letter? Did you end it with a punctuation mark? If not, be sure to fix it.

Match the common noun with the proper noun.

(1) holiday   Whiskers
(2) cat   Bible
(3) city   Ohio
(4) park   Christmas
(5) book   Yellowstone
(6) state   Boston

Language Level 3 – Lesson 2

Name_____   Exercise 3   Day 8

Calendar

Let's look at how we use a calendar to keep track of days, weeks, and months.

March 2020						
Sun.	Mon.	Tues.	Wed.	Thurs.	Fri.	Sat.
1	2	3	4	5	6	7
8	9	10	11	12	13	14
15	16	17	18	19	20	21
22	23	24	25	26	27	28
29	30	31				

- Have the student answer the questions as you study the calendar together.

- Name the days of the week.
- What day of the week is March 20th?
- How many days fall on a Wednesday in March 2020?
- How many days are in March 2020?

Do you remember the months of the year? Say them to your teacher.

There is a little rhyme on the next page that can help us keep track of how many days are in each month. Practice this rhyme with your teacher until you have it memorized.

Language Level 3 – Lesson 2

> 30 days has September,
> April, June, and November
> All the rest have 31
> Except for February
> Which has 28
> But 29 in a leap year

TEACHER NOTE • The poem can be found in the back of the book for the student to use for practice.

Match the months to how many days it has. **Note:** February is tricky! It has two answers.

(1) January
(2) February
(3) March
(4) April
(5) May
(6) June
(7) July
(8) August
(9) September
(10) October
(11) November
(12) December

28

29

30

31

Name_____   Exercise 4   Day 9

 **READING COMPREHENSION**

Read pages 12–13 of *101 Favorite Stories from the Bible* with your teacher.

Answer the questions on page 13.

Copy Psalm 139:14, then memorize it with your teacher.

Copy the picture on page 13 and color it. Draw the whole picture or just choose one or two things from the picture. Copy the caption from page 13 below.

Language Level 3 – Lesson 2

Name_____   Exercise 5   Day 10

 **Short -i, -o, and -u Sound Words**

We are going to work with words that make the short -i, -o, and -u sound.

Learn to spell these words:

admit, adopt, doctor, drink, lunch,
pond, slip, such, under, until

Write the spelling words in the correct boxes.

(1)   (6)
(2)   (7)
(3)   (8)
(4)   (9)
(5)   (10)

Write a fun sentence using at least two of your spelling words. Be sure to start your sentence with a capital letter and end it with a punctuation mark.

Language Level 3 – Lesson 2   35

Exercise 5 — Day 10

Write your spelling words on notecards. Write one word on each card. You may create right-brain flashcards with your words.

Optional Activities

- If student needs more practice, you may assign these additional activities.

Write your spelling words.

(1) _____   (6) _____

(2) _____   (7) _____

(3) _____   (8) _____

(4) _____   (9) _____

(5) _____   (10) _____

Ask your teacher to read each spelling word. Spell the word out loud to your teacher and use it in a sentence.

Lesson 3

The Sabbath

Mr. Lopez started the class by reminding the students of their celebration the previous week. He explained that there are lots of celebrations in the Bible. "The Sabbath is a day that God set aside for us to rest and worship Him. It is a day to celebrate God's blessings." He then asked the class to open their Bible to Genesis 2:2–3. He read, "² By the seventh day God completed His work which He had done, and He rested on the seventh day from all His work which He had done. ³ Then God blessed the seventh day and sanctified it, because in it He rested from all His work which God had created and made."

Mr. Lopez asked where else in the Bible the Sabbath is mentioned. Micah raised his hand. When Mr. Lopez called on him, he said quietly, "It is in the Ten Commandments, and Jesus talked about it, too!" Mr. Lopez agreed and said that the Sabbath was mentioned so many times in the Bible, they wouldn't have time to read all the verses, even if they spent the whole class reading them! The class turned to the Ten Commandments in Exodus 20. Mr. Lopez read verse 8, "Remember the sabbath day, to keep it holy." As the class was dismissed, Mr. Lopez challenged the students to find out what Jesus had to say about the Sabbath. Micah, Claire, and all the students were eager to study and talk about it in next week's class.

NARRATION PRACTICE

(1) How did Mr. Lopez start the class?

(2) What did the students learn about?

(3) What were the students going to study before the next class?

Name _____   Exercise 1   Day 11

Copy Work

 **TEACHER NOTE** • We have used the NASB version. You may use any version you prefer for the student to copy.

Copy Genesis 2:3 below.

"Then God blessed the seventh day and sanctified it, because in it He rested from all His work which God had created and made."

Sight Words

Practice the sight words using your memorization cards.

Language Level 3 – Lesson 3

Name _____ Exercise 2 Day 12

 **Pronouns**

Do you remember what a *proper noun* is? It names a noun. The word "I" is a special type of proper noun called a pronoun. A *pronoun* takes the place of a noun. We use a capital letter whenever we use the word "I" in a sentence.

Write a sentence using "I" as a pronoun:
_____
_____
_____
_____

We are going to study singular and plural pronouns.

Singular means one. *Plural* means more than one.

Singular pronouns:

> I   me   you   he   him   she   her   it

Plural pronouns:

> we   they   them   us

Write the correct pronoun that can take the place of the underlined noun.

(1) Mr. Lopez started the class. _____

(2) Claire read her Bible. _____

(3) Micah and Claire were late for class. _____

Language Level 3 – Lesson 3

Exercise 2 — Day 12

Circle the pronouns in the sentences:

(4) I will give you an apple.

(5) He will say a prayer before lunch.

(6) Hand me the cup.

(7) Pass the plates to them.

(8) They will enjoy the meal.

(9) We are full.

(10) She sent us to wash the dishes.

Write a sentence using a plural pronoun:
_____
_____

Language Level 3 – Lesson 3

Name_____   Exercise **3**   Day 13

Days of the Week

Do you remember the days of the week? Say them to your teacher. Abbreviate means to shorten. We can abbreviate the names of the week. Copy the names of the week and their abbreviations.

Sunday _____   Sun. _____

Monday _____   Mon. _____

Tuesday _____   Tues. _____

Wednesday _____   Wed. _____

Thursday _____   Thurs. _____

Friday _____   Fri. _____

Saturday _____   Sat. _____

Language Level 3 – Lesson 3

Name _____   Exercise 4   Day 14

 **READING COMPREHENSION**

Read pages 14–15 of *101 Favorite Stories from the Bible* with your teacher.

Answer the questions on page 15.

Copy Romans 5:19, then memorize it with your teacher.

Copy the picture on page 15 and color it. Draw the whole picture or only the people. Copy the caption from page 15 below.

Language Level 3 – Lesson 3

Name _____ Exercise 5 Day 15

 **Spelling Practice**

Long -a Sound Words

We are going to work with long -a pattern words.

Learn to spell these words:

> away, pray, today, brain, nail,
> raise, sail, game, state, take

Put the spelling words in alphabetical order using the first letter of each word. If the first letters of the words are the same, use the second letter to put them in order.

Use the alphabet below to help you put the words in order. If you are not sure how to do this, ask your teacher for help.

a b c d e f g h i j k l m n o p q r s t u v w x y z

(1) _____   (6) _____

(2) _____   (7) _____

(3) _____   (8) _____

(4) _____   (9) _____

(5) _____   (10) _____

Language Level 3 – Lesson 3   43

Exercise 5 — Day 15

Write a fun sentence using at least two of your spelling words. Be sure to start your sentence with a capital letter and end it with a punctuation mark.

_____
_____
_____
_____

Write your spelling words on notecards. Write one word on each card. You may create right-brain flashcards with your words.

Optional Activities

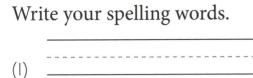
- If student needs more practice, you may assign these additional activities.

Write your spelling words.

(1) _____ (6) _____

(2) _____ (7) _____

(3) _____ (8) _____

(4) _____ (9) _____

(5) _____ (10) _____

Ask your teacher to read each spelling word. Spell the word out loud to your teacher and use it in a sentence.

Language Level 3 – Lesson 3

Cecily Parsley's Nursery Rhymes

Beatrix Potter

We have a little garden,
A garden of our own,
And every day we water there
The seeds that we have sown.

We love our little garden,
And tend it with such care,
You will not find a faded leaf
Or blighted blossom there.

Comprehension

Were there any words you didn't understand? Circle them.

- The teacher should go over with the student the meaning of the circled words in the context of the poem.

(1) Who wrote the poem?

(2) What is the poem about?

(3) Each section of the poem is called a stanza. There are two stanzas in this poem. Which stanza is your favorite? Why?

(4) Explain how this poem makes you feel.

https://www.gutenberg.org/files/23350/23350-h/23350-h.htm

Name _____ Exercise 1 Day 16

Memorization

Memorize your favorite stanza of this poem. Can you memorize the whole poem?

- Both the teacher and the student should work together to memorize the stanza.

Sight Words

Practice sight words using your memorization cards.

 **Butterfly Fun**

My garden is full of butterflies. Find two identical ones. Color them the same. Color the rest of the butterflies differently.

Language Level 3 – Lesson 4

Name_____   Exercise 2   Day 17

Plural Nouns -s, -es

One of something is called a *singular* noun.

More than one of something is called a *plural* noun.

Do you remember how we make a plural noun by adding -s and -es to the end of a word? Many nouns can be made plural by adding -s.

If the noun ends in -s, -ss, -sh, -ch, or -x, we add -es to the end to make it plural.

Remember:

| plural = add -s | ends in s, ss, sh, ch, or x = add -es |

Add -s or -es to the end of the words to make them plural.

(1) bus_____   (5) smile_____

(2) orphan_____   (6) bush_____

(3) church_____   (7) hand_____

(4) box_____   (8) mess_____

Write a sentence using a plural noun.

_____
_____
_____
_____

Language Level 3 – Lesson 4   47

Name_____   Exercise **3**   Day 18

Months of the Year

Do you remember the months of the year? Say them to your teacher.

Do you remember what abbreviate means? Yes, it means to shorten. We can abbreviate the months of the year just like we did for the days of the week.

Copy the months of the year and their abbreviations. Some months cannot be abbreviated.

January _____	Jan. _____
February _____	Feb. _____
March _____	Mar. _____
April _____	Apr. _____
May _____	
June _____	
July _____	
August _____	Aug. _____
September _____	Sept. _____
October _____	Oct. _____
November _____	Nov. _____
December _____	Dec. _____

48 Language Level 3 – Lesson 4

Name_____   Exercise 3   Day 18

 Use your finger to trace the road in front of the blue bus, yellow car, and red car.

See if you can answer the following questions. Be sure to tell your teacher the answer.

(1) Which car ends up at the drive-in for a hamburger?

(2) Which ends up at the ball field?

(3) Which one will end up at the pool?

Language Level 3 – Lesson 4

Exercise 4 — Day 19

 **READING COMPREHENSION**

Read pages 16–17 of *101 Favorite Stories from the Bible* with your teacher.

Answer the questions on page 17.

Copy Genesis 1:28, then memorize it with your teacher.

Copy the picture on page 17 and color it. Draw the whole picture or only the people. Copy the caption from page 17 below.

Name_____   Exercise 5 Day 20

Long -e Sound Words

We are going to work with words with the long -e pattern.

Learn to spell these words:

> baby, breeze, clean, easy, keep,
> meal, need, seat, sleep, theme

(1) Find the spelling words in the word search. Look across and down.

- baby
- breeze
- clean
- easy
- keep
- meal
- need
- seat
- sleep
- theme

```
V S U X M B I U M Q S T
H L Q O E N R N Q X E H
S E T W A E N B Z C A E
K E E P L E H A U S T M
U P C N R D G B H P Q E
M T E A S Y V Y O O I Y
G O N T S B R E E Z E A
B T C L E A N B R S L I
M E J A Z K L E S P D C
```

Language Level 3 – Lesson 4   51

Exercise 5 Day 20

Write a fun sentence using at least two of your spelling words. Be sure to start your sentence with a capital letter and end it with a punctuation mark.

_____
_____
_____
_____

Write your spelling words on notecards. Write one word on each card. You may create right-brain flashcards with your words.

Optional Activities

TEACHER NOTE • If student needs more practice, you may assign these additional activities.

Write your spelling words.

(1) _____   (6) _____

(2) _____   (7) _____

(3) _____   (8) _____

(4) _____   (9) _____

(5) _____   (10) _____

Ask your teacher to read each spelling word. Spell the word out loud to your teacher and use it in a sentence.

CREATE YOUR OWN DICTIONARY!

Lesson 5

The Trumpet

What was that loud sound? It sounded almost like a trumpet. It got louder as the children walked closer to their Sunday School class. Micah and Claire were surprised to see Mr. Lopez blowing into a strange looking horn. Mr. Lopez stopped and explained that he was blowing into a ram's horn, also called a shofar. People in Bible times blew the horn to get the attention of people near and far. The priests also blew the shofar to signal a holy day, where we get our word holiday. Micah whispered to Claire, "Wow! That sure would get my attention!"

Mr. Lopez went on to explain that there was a special day on which God told the priests to blow the shofar. God didn't give this day a name, but it became known as the Feast of Trumpets. The people were to rest on this day, just like they would if it were the Sabbath. In Leviticus 23, God says that this day was to be a day to remember, but it does not say what the people were to remember. Mr. Lopez said that he likes to remember on this day all the ways God has been faithful to him and his family.

Mr. Lopez told the class that some people celebrate this day by eating apple slices dipped in honey. As he handed out the special snack, Claire told Micah she thought this was a strange way to celebrate. Micah agreed, but they both enjoyed their sweet apple treat.

(1) What did the children hear on their way to class?

(2) What holiday did Mr. Lopez teach the class about?

(3) How did the class celebrate?

Name _____   Exercise 1   Day 21

Memorization

 • We have used the NASB version. You may use any version you prefer.

Mr. Lopez told the class that the Feast of Trumpets is described in Leviticus 23:24.

"Speak to the sons of Israel, saying, 'In the seventh month on the first of the month you shall have a rest, a reminder by blowing of trumpets, a holy convocation.'"

Memorize the verse with your teacher.

Grouping

Which word in each row doesn't belong? Circle it.

(1)	jump	toss	ball	run
(2)	horse	cow	goat	lion
(3)	shoe	puzzle	frisbee	ball
(4)	flower	rose	tulip	peony

Sight Words

Do you know all the sight words yet? If not, keep practicing them with your teacher at least once a week.

54   Language Level 3 – Lesson 5

Name_____   Exercise 2   Day 22

 **Plural Nouns**

We are going to work with more plural nouns. Do you remember what a plural noun is? Yes, more than one person, place, or thing. Study the examples:

vowel + y, add -s	vowel + o, add -s	consonant + o, add -es
key = keys	radio = radios	hero = heroes

Add -s or -es to the end of the words to make them plural. Study the examples if you aren't sure.

(1) toy_____   (4) tomato_____

(2) tornado_____   (5) patio_____

(3) zoo_____   (6) monkey_____

There are two exceptions to this rule!

   piano = pianos   photo = photos

Write the two plural words that are exceptions.
_____   _____

Write a sentence using two of the plural words we studied.
_____
_____

Language Level 3 – Lesson 5   55

Types of Sentences

Do you remember the different kinds of punctuation we use at the end of a sentence? Yes, we use a period, question mark, or an exclamation point at the end of a sentence.

There are four types of sentences. You may need to ask your teacher to help you read their names. They are:

Imperative: This type of sentence is a command and ends with a period.

Declarative: This type of sentence is a statement and ends with a period, too.

Exclamatory: This type of sentence is an exclamation and has emotion. It ends in an exclamation point.

Interrogative: This is a big word that means a question. This type of sentence ends with a question mark.

What kind of sentences are these?

Put an **IM** for Imperative, **D** for Declarative, **E** for Exclamatory, and **IN** for Interrogative:

(1) ____ Why did the priest blow the shofar?

(2) ____ I like apple slices dipped in honey.

(3) ____ Stop that dog!

(4) ____ Bring me that book.

Exercise 3 — Day 23

Interjections

An interjection is a word that expresses emotion or feelings. Often, it is found at the beginning of a sentence and followed with an exclamation point. Here is an example:

Wow! I read the whole book today.

Circle the interjections in each sentence.

(5) Oops! I dropped the plate.

(6) Oh, were you in line?

(7) Hey! Don't touch the hot stove.

Write a sentence using an interjection.

_____
_____
_____
_____
_____

Language Level 3 – Lesson 5

Name_____ Exercise 4 Day 24

 **READING COMPREHENSION**

Read pages 18–19 of *101 Favorite Stories from the Bible* with your teacher.

Answer the questions on page 19.

Copy Psalm 5:4, then memorize it with your teacher.

Copy the picture on page 19 and color it. Draw the whole picture or only the people. Copy the caption from page 19 below.

Language Level 3 – Lesson 5

Name_____   Exercise **5**   Day 25

 **Long -i Sound Words**

We are going to work with words with the long -i pattern.

Learn to spell these words:

> bike, child, dime, hydrant, July,
> light, pilot, quiet, sigh, sign

Create your own word search with your spelling words. Follow the example.

Put spelling words in puzzle

D	O	G		
				F
H	O	T		O
				X
S		M	O	M	M
O					O
B		P	O	T		P

Fill in rest of the boxes with letters

D	O	G	W	K	V	A
C	Z	L	I	U	F	C
H	O	T	B	S	O	R
B	Z	E	Y	P	X	Y
U	R	V	Z	H	H	F
S	W	M	O	M	U	M
O	O	B	O	O	T	O
B	W	P	O	T	O	P

Write a fun sentence using at least two of your spelling words. Be sure to start your sentence with a capital letter and end it with a punctuation mark.

_____
_____
_____
_____

Language Level 3 – Lesson 5   59

Exercise 5   Day 25

Write your spelling words on notecards. Write one word on each card. You may create right-brain flashcards with your words.

Optional Activities

 • If student needs more practice, you may assign these additional activities.

Write your spelling words.

(1) _____   (6) _____

(2) _____   (7) _____

(3) _____   (8) _____

(4) _____   (9) _____

(5) _____   (10) _____

Ask your teacher to read each spelling word. Spell the word out loud to your teacher and use it in a sentence.

 **PICTURE STUDY**

Lesson 6

Title: *Mouse on a Summer Day*
Artist: Kocchisan

 **OBSERVATION SKILLS**

(1) Who is the artist of this picture?

(2) What is the mouse doing?

(3) What things do you see in the picture?

(4) What colors are used in this picture?

(5) How does this picture make you feel?

Name _____ Exercise 1 Day 26

Story Writing

Finish this story about the mouse in the picture.

It was a warm summer day when the mouse found a field of dandelion flowers gone to seed.

Language Level 3 – Lesson 6

Name_____   Exercise 2   Day 27

 **Plural Nouns**

Do you remember what a plural noun is? Yes, a plural noun means more than one person, place, or thing.

Consonant + y

If the noun ends in a consonant + y, we change the y to an i and add -es to the end to make it plural.

party = parties   baby = babies

F or Fe

If the noun ends in an f or fe, we change the f or fe to a v and add -es to the end to make it plural.

wolf = wolves   life = lives

Change these words to make them plural.

(1) city _____   (3) country _____

(2) leaf _____   (4) knife _____

There are two exceptions to this rule!

   roof = roofs   cliff = cliffs

Write the two words that are exceptions.

_____   _____

Language Level 3 – Lesson 6

Name _____   Exercise 3   Day 28

Commas

We use commas when we write a list of things in a sentence. A comma comes after each item in a list. Study the commas in this sentence and then circle them:

> The mouse looked at the grass, clouds, and the night sky.

Write a sentence with a list separated by commas.

_____
_____
_____

We also use a comma when we address someone. When the person's name is first in a sentence, the comma goes after the name:

> Claire, please bring the apples here.

When the name comes in the middle of the sentence, a comma goes before and after the name:

> You, God, are worthy of praise.

When the name comes at the end of the sentence, a comma goes before the name:

> Bring the honey over here, Micah.

Put a comma where they go in the sentences.

(1) I am going to read about the Sabbath, Micah.
(2) Claire, did you memorize the verse?
(3) What, God, did you want us to remember?

Write a sentence addressing someone.
_____
_____
_____
_____

Did you start your sentences with a capital letter and end them with punctuation? Did you correctly use commas? If not, be sure to fix the mistakes.

Name _____   Exercise 4   Day 29

 **READING COMPREHENSION**

Read pages 20–21 of *101 Favorite Stories from the Bible* with your teacher.

Answer the questions on page 21.

Copy Luke 1:51, then memorize it with your teacher.

Copy the picture on page 21 and color it. Draw the whole picture or only the people. Copy the caption from page 21 below.

Language Level 3 – Lesson 6

Name_____   Exercise 5 Day 30

 **Long -o Sound Words**

We are going to work with words with the long -o pattern.

Learn to spell these words:

> alone, cold, grow, hope, moan,
> most, open, road, woke, yellow

Write the spelling words in the correct boxes.

(1)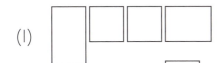

(2)

(3)

(4)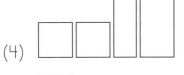

(5)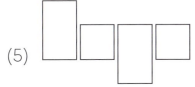

(6)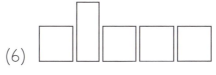

(7)

(8)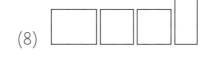

(9)

(10)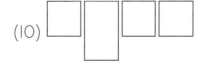

Write a fun sentence using at least two of your spelling words. Be sure to start your sentence with a capital letter and end it with a punctuation mark.

_____
_____
_____
_____

Language Level 3 – Lesson 6

Exercise 5 — Day 30

Write your spelling words on notecards. Write one word on each card. You may create right-brain flashcards with your words.

Optional Activities

- If student needs more practice, you may assign these additional activities.

Write your spelling words.

(1) _____ (6) _____

(2) _____ (7) _____

(3) _____ (8) _____

(4) _____ (9) _____

(5) _____ (10) _____

Ask your teacher to read each spelling word. Spell the word out loud to your teacher and use it in a sentence.

Day of Atonement

Mr. Lopez asked the class what the Sabbath is. Claire raised her hand and said, "It is a day of rest!" Mr. Lopez agreed. He said that God told the Israelites they were to have a special Sabbath called the Day of Atonement. Atonement is a fancy word that means "covering." This was to be a special day, but very serious. This day would help the people understand what was to come when Jesus died on the cross to pay for our sins.

Mr. Lopez looked sad as he told the children about how the priests would take a goat and sacrifice it for the sin of the people. They would take another goat and let it go free in the wilderness. One goat gave up its life so that the other goat could go free. Micah raised his hand. "Mr. Lopez, isn't that what Jesus did for us? He gave up his life so that we could be forgiven and free to go to heaven." Mr. Lopez said, "Exactly, Micah! Jesus paid the price for our sins and has risen from the dead. We no longer sacrifice animals for our sin. The animal sacrifice was like a cover over our sin, but Jesus paid for our sin in full."

Mr. Lopez ended the class by saying that the Day of Atonement is a holy day set apart once a year. "It is a good day to think about the cost of sin and to thank God for sending Jesus." The children quietly left the class, thinking about Jesus and the Day of Atonement.

(1) What holy day is this story about?

(2) What did the children learn about this day?

(3) What can we be thankful for on this day?

- You may read more about the Day of Atonement in Leviticus 23:26-32.

Syllables

Words can be split up into syllables, or sounds.

Ask your teacher to say the following words and clap for each syllable.

One-Syllable Words:

Claire, class, God

Two-Syllable Words:

Micah, special, thanking

Three-Syllable Words:

atonement, covering, understand

Do you hear the syllables? Now it is your turn. Ask your teacher to say the words again and clap for each syllable, but this time, you clap, too!

How did you do? Did you hear the syllables? This time, you read the words to your teacher and clap for each syllable.

Name_____   Exercise 2 Day 32

 **Irregular Plural Nouns**

Some plural nouns don't follow the rules! They are called *irregular nouns*.

Read this list of nouns. You will need to remember how to make each of these words plural.

Single	Plural	Single	Plural
man	men	goose	geese
woman	women	mouse	mice
child	children	ox	oxen
person	people	octopus	octopi
		cactus	cacti

Single	Plural	Single	Plural
deer	deer	moose	moose
fish	fish	corn	corn
sheep	sheep	seaweed	seaweed

Exercise 2 — Day 32

Write the plural form of each word. Try to remember it before looking at the previous page.

(1) cactus _____

(2) child _____

(3) corn _____

(4) deer _____

(5) fish _____

(6) goose _____

(7) man _____

(8) moose _____

(9) mouse _____

(10) octopus _____

(11) ox _____

(12) person _____

(13) seaweed _____

(14) sheep _____

(15) woman _____

Language Level 3 – Lesson 7

Name_____ Exercise 3 Day 33

Initials

The first letter in a word is called the initial letter. Initial means first. Initial letters of a name are called *initials*. We use a period after an initial. We may use initials for the first, middle, or last name of a person.

Example: The abbreviation for Abraham Lincoln is A. L.

Write your initials. _____

Write these presidents' names using initials for their name.

(1) John Quincy Adams _____

(2) William Howard Taft _____

Titles

We can abbreviate (shorten) many titles. A title describes a person, their job, or their position. Titles begin with a capital letter. We put a period at the end of an abbreviation.

> Mister is the title of a man.
> Miss is the title of an unmarried woman.
> Missus is the title of a married woman.

Write three sentences using Mr., Ms., and Mrs.

Mr. _____

Ms. _____

Mrs. _____

Language Level 3 – Lesson 7

Exercise 3 — Day 33

Match the titles to the correct abbreviations.

(3) Mister   Ms.
(4) Miss   Mrs.
(5) Missus   Mr.

(6) Doctor   Det.
(7) Reverend   Prof.
(8) Detective   Dr.
(9) Professor   Rev.

(10) Honorable   Sen.
(11) Senator   Pres.
(12) Representative Hon.
(13) President   Rep.

(14) Captain   Sgt.
(15) General   Capt.
(16) Sergeant   Gen.

Language Level 3 – Lesson 7

Name_____   Exercise 4   Day 34

 **READING COMPREHENSION**

Read pages 22–23 of *101 Favorite Stories from the Bible* with your teacher.

Answer the questions on page 23.

Copy Hebrews 11:8, then memorize it with your teacher.

Copy the picture on page 23 and color it. Draw the whole picture or only the people. Copy the caption from page 23 below.

Language Level 3 – Lesson 7

Name_____   Exercise 5   Day 35

 **Long -u Sound Words**

We are going to work with words with the long -u pattern.

Learn to spell these words:

> grew, huge, juice, music, newt,
> noon, root, took, truth, tune

Write a funny story using as many spelling words as you can in each sentence.

_____
_____
_____
_____
_____
_____
_____
_____
_____
_____
_____
_____

Circle the spelling words you used in your sentences.

Write your spelling words on notecards. Write one word on each card. You may create right-brain flashcards with your words.

76   Language Level 3 – Lesson 7

Lesson 8

Psalm 20

May the Lord answer you in the day of trouble!
May the name of the God of Jacob set you *securely* on high!
² May He send you help from the sanctuary
And support you from Zion!
³ May He remember all your meal offerings
And find your burnt offering acceptable! Selah.

⁴ May He grant you your heart's desire
And fulfill all your counsel!
⁵ We will sing for joy over your victory,
And in the name of our God we will set up our banners.
May the Lord fulfill all your petitions.

⁶ Now I know that the Lord saves His anointed;
He will answer him from His holy heaven
With the saving strength of His right hand.
⁷ Some *boast* in chariots and some in horses,
But we will boast in the name of the Lord, our God.
⁸ They have bowed down and fallen,
But we have risen and stood upright.
⁹ Save, O Lord;
May the King answer us in the day we call.

Comprehension

A Psalm is a song. There are 150 Psalms in the Bible. Many of them were written by David, including this Psalm.

- Please review tips on Reading Psalms at the beginning of the book.
- The teacher should go over with the student the meaning of the circled words in the context of the Psalm.

It is not known for sure what the word "selah" means. Some think it means to pause. We can use it as a reminder to stop and think about what was said.

Were there any words you didn't understand? Circle them.

Language Level 3 – Lesson 8   77

Name _____ Exercise 1 Day 36

 **NARRATION PRACTICE**

(1) What chapter of Psalms did you read?

(2) How many verses are there in this chapter?

(3) What was this Psalm about?

(4) What did you learn about God in this Psalm?

(5) What were your favorite verses?

Memorization

Memorize at least three verses of this poem. The verses should be in a row and may be picked by you or your teacher.

 **OBSERVATION SKILLS**

(1) Circle the sentence that is true:

The fox is asleep.   The fox is hungry.

The fox is thirsty.   The fox is happy.

Language Level 3 – Lesson 8

Name _____   Exercise 2   Day 37

 **Possessive Nouns**

A possessive noun shows who or what owns or has something.

Do you remember what singular means? It means one of something.

We make a singular noun possessive by adding an apostrophe and an -s. Here is an example from our Psalm:

May He grant you your heart's desire.

You have one heart. In this sentence, we want to show the heart "owning" or possessing what it desires.

We show it is a possessive noun by adding an apostrophe and an -s to the word *heart*.

Fill in the blank with a possessive noun.

The _____ room was clean.

The _____ dog was lost.

There is an exception to this rule! *Its* is a singular possessive noun, but it does not have an apostrophe. Only the contraction *it's* has an apostrophe.

Remember, a contraction is when two words are shortened into one, with an apostrophe in place of the missing letters.

Write *it's* or *its* correctly in the sentences.

(1) The mouse lost _____ cheese.

(2) _____ under the couch.

Language Level 3 – Lesson 8

Exercise 2   Day 37

When a plural noun ends in an -s we show ownership by adding only an apostrophe to the end of the word. Study this example:

The dogs' food was almost gone.

This sentence shows us that there is more than one dog whose food is almost gone.

We added an apostrophe to the end of the plural noun "dogs."

Fill in the blank with a plural possessive noun.

The _____ toys are in the box.

The _____ eggs were about to hatch.

Fill in the blank with the correct word.

dogs   dog's   dogs'

(3) The _____ bone was heavy.

(4) The _____ bowls were the same.

(5) The _____ were playing.

Name _____ Exercise 3 Day 38

 **Sentences: Subject and Predicate**

Sentences can split into two parts: a subject and a predicate.

The subject = who or what the sentence is about
The predicate = what the subject does or is

Example:

The fox is sleeping.

The *subject* is: The fox

The *predicate* is: is sleeping.

The fox is what this sentence is about. What is the subject doing? It is sleeping.

Underline the subject of each sentence. Circle the predicate in each sentence.

(1) The cat caught a mouse.

(2) The fox played in the field.

When a sentence has more than one subject, we say it is has a compound subject. Study the example:

The dog and cat ran around the tree.

The sentence has two subjects: the *dog* and the *cat*

Write a sentence with a compound subject.

_____
_____
_____
_____

Language Level 3 – Lesson 8

Exercise 3 — Day 38

When a predicate has more than one verb, we say the sentence has a compound predicate. Study the example:

The fox ran and jumped into the hole.

The sentence has two verbs: *ran* and *jumped*

Write a sentence with a compound predicate.
_____
_____

Name_____   Exercise 4   Day 39

 **READING COMPREHENSION**

Read pages 24–25 of *101 Favorite Stories from the Bible* with your teacher.

Answer the questions on page 25.

Copy Matthew 10:37b, then memorize it with your teacher.

Copy the picture on page 25 and color it. Draw the whole picture or only the people. Copy the caption from page 25 below.

Language Level 3 – Lesson 8

Name _____   Exercise 5   Day 40

 **Sight Words**

Learn to spell these words:

> seven, about, today, laugh, done, myself, start, eight, much, shall

Put the spelling words in alphabetical order. If you find two words that start with the same letter, look at the second letter in each of the words to see which goes first.

(1) _____   (6) _____

(2) _____   (7) _____

(3) _____   (8) _____

(4) _____   (9) _____

(5) _____   (10) _____

Write a fun sentence using at least two of your spelling words. Be sure to start your sentence with a capital letter and end it with a punctuation mark.

_____

_____

Write your spelling words on notecards. Write one word on each card. You may create right-brain flashcards with your words.

84   Language Level 3 – Lesson 8

 **Lesson 9**

Feast of Tabernacles

The children were curious about the tent sitting next to Mr. Lopez's desk. Mr. Lopez settled the class down and read from Leviticus 23 about the Feast of Tabernacles. He explained that a tabernacle is a temporary place to live. It is like a tent, except it is made from branches. He said the first and eighth day of this feast is a Sabbath.

At a set time every fall, the people were to live in their tent for seven days to remind them of when God brought the Israelites out of Egypt, where they were slaves. Mr. Lopez reminded the children that we all were once a slave to sin. When Jesus paid for our sin and we accept Him, we start on a journey of following the Lord, just like the Israelites did in the wilderness. He also reminded the children that we are on a journey to heaven. This world is only our temporary place to live, just like when we stay in a tent. Jesus said He is preparing a permanent home for us in heaven.

Mr. Lopez shared some interesting things about the Feast of Tabernacles. He said that it is possible the pilgrims celebrated this holy week in what we now call Thanksgiving. He said some people think Jesus was born during this feast week. Jesus celebrated the Feast of Tabernacles, and Zechariah 14:16 says that someday, all nations will celebrate this feast! Once again, Mr. Lopez had given the children a lot to think about as they left their class.

(1) What holy week is this story about?
(2) How were the people supposed to celebrate this holy week?
(3) Why do you think Mr. Lopez had a tent next to his desk?
(4) What were the interesting things Mr. Lopez shared about the Feast of Tabernacles?

Name _____   Exercise 1   Day 41

Rhyming

Write a word that rhymes with each word. Remember, rhyming words have the same ending sound. The ending does not have to be spelled the same.

dog _____   rest _____

name _____   blue _____

jump _____   time _____

sew _____   take _____

Write two sentences end with a rhyme. You may use the rhyming words above.

_____
_____
_____
_____
_____
_____

Name_____   Exercise 2   Day 42

1st Quarter Review
(Each question is 4 points)

TEACHER NOTE • Give student access to the Study Sheets in the back of the book while completing this Review.

a b c d e f g h i j k l m n o p q r s t u v w x y z

(1) Circle the vowels in the alphabet.

(2) Underline the consonants in the alphabet

Match the common noun with the proper noun.

(3) holiday   Fido
(4) dog   Bible
(5) city   Kentucky
(6) park   Christmas
(7) book   Yellowstone
(8) state   Cleveland

Circle the pronouns in the sentences:

(9) He will say a prayer before lunch.

(10) Hand me the cup.

(11) They will enjoy the meal.

(12) We are full.

Language Level 3 – Lesson 9

Exercise 2 — Day 42

Add -s or -es to the end of the words to make them plural.

(13) church _____   (14) toy _____

Change these words to make them plural.

(15) city _____   (16) leaf _____

Write the plural form of each word.

(17) child _____   (20) deer _____

(18) goose _____   (21) man _____

(19) person _____

Fill in the blank with a possessive noun.

(22) The _____ room was clean.

Write *it's* or *its* correctly in the sentences.

(23) The mouse lost _____ cheese.

(24) _____ under the couch.

Fill in the blank with a plural possessive noun.

(25) The _____ eggs were about to hatch.

88   Language Level 3 – Lesson 9

Name _____ Exercise 3 Day 43

1st Quarter Review
(Each question is 4 points)

 **Teacher Note:** Give student access to the Study Sheets in the back of the book while completing this Review.

(1) Write a sentence that asks a question.

_____
- -
_____

(2) Say the days of the week to your teacher.

(3) Say the months of the year to your teacher.

Match the months to how many days it has. **Note:** February is tricky! It has two answers.

(4) January

(5) February

(6) March

(7) April   28

(8) May

(9) June   29

(10) July

                    30

(11) August

(12) September   31

(13) October

(14) November

(15) December

Language Level 3 – Lesson 9

Label the sentences. Put an **IM** for Imperative, **D** for Declarative, **E** for Exclamatory and **IN** for Interrogative:

(16) _____ Why did the priest blow the shofar?

(17) _____ I like apple slices dipped in honey.

(18) _____ Stop that dog!

(19) _____ Bring me that book.

(20) Write a sentence using an interjection.

_____
_____
_____
_____

(21) Write a sentence addressing someone.

_____
_____
_____
_____

(22) Write your initials. _____

Write the correct abbreviations.

(23) Mister _____ (24) Missus _____

Underline the subject of the sentence. Circle the predicate of the sentence.

(25) The cat caught a mouse.

90 Language Level 3 – Lesson 9

Name _____   Exercise 4   Day 44

 **READING COMPREHENSION**

Read pages 26–27 of *101 Favorite Stories from the Bible* with your teacher.

Answer the questions on page 27.

Copy Psalm 145:18, then memorize it with your teacher.

Copy the picture on page 27 and color it. Draw the whole picture or only the people. Copy the caption from page 27 below.

Language Level 3 – Lesson 9

Name_____   Exercise 5   Day 45

 **Spelling Review**

Use your flashcards to practice your spelling words.

You may:

- Ask someone to quiz you on how to spell the words
- Play spelling games found in the back of the book
- Create your own spelling games
- Use each word in a sentence and say them to your teacher

Students may choose their own spelling words this week for their dictionary. They may add their words to the spelling words section in the back of the book.

Tell your teacher a story about what you see in this picture.

Language Level 3 – Lesson 9

Lesson 10

Giving Thanks

Thanksgiving was coming soon. It was Micah's favorite holiday. In years past, it meant turkey, mashed potatoes, buttery rolls, and three kinds of pie! But this year would be different.

Over the last few weeks, their Sunday school class had learned how God watched over Israel in Bible times, even when their situation seemed hopeless. They also learned how the Israelites showed their thankfulness to God during special feast days.

Mr. Lopez explained that God still watches over us today. He mentioned the kids in the orphanage and how there were lots of people working together to take care of them. He said that today, God often blesses and provides through other people. He called that being the "hands and feet" of Jesus.

He asked the class to think about ways that God has blessed them through other people.

Claire shared about the time she broke her arm. She was grateful for the doctors and nurses that helped her that day.

Ava said that lots of friends from the church brought meals to her family when her Mom was in the hospital.

Micah thought of Carlos and the other kids at the orphanage. He realized what a blessing it was to get to live with his parents.

Everyone began to see different ways that God watches over us today. After all the kids had shared, Mr. Lopez challenged them to think of ways they could show their gratitude to God this Thanksgiving and to bring their ideas to class next Sunday.

(1) What holiday is this story about?

(2) What did Mr. Lopez mean about being the "hands and feet" of Jesus?

(3) What were the children thankful for?

Language Level 3 – Lesson 10

Name_____   Exercise 1   Day 46

Maps and Direction: Find Your Way!

Maps often show you which way is north, south, east or west. These help you to find your way when you are looking for some place. Look at this map and see if you can answer the questions below. Be sure to tell your teacher the answer.

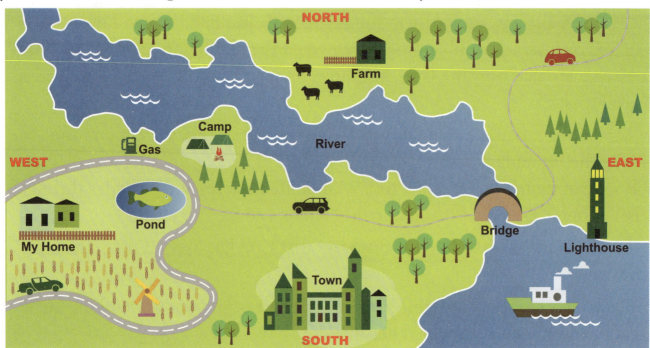

(1) Is the pond west or east of the bridge?

(2) Is the farm north or south of the road?

(3) Which way is the red car driving?

(4) The town is _____ of the camp.

(5) The ship is _____ of the bridge.

(6) Which car is closest to the camp?

(7) Which car is on the north part of the map?

(8) Where are the cows on the map?

(9) The gas station is on the east or west side of the map?

(10) Is the lighthouse on the east or west side of the map?

Language Level 3 – Lesson 10

Name_____ Exercise 2 Day 47

 **Action Verbs**

An action verb tells what is happening in a sentence.

Study the example:

Claire runs to class.

(1) Circle the verb in the sentence above.

Action verbs can tell something that is happening now or something that has already happened. We can change our example to take place in the past:

Claire ran to class.

(2) Circle the verb in the sentence above.

Sometimes we can add the suffix -ed to a verb to show it happened in the past. Study the example:

Mom called Claire for lunch.

(3) Circle the verb in the sentence above.

Write a sentence for each verb. Then write a sentence showing something happened in the past. You will need to change the verb!

wait

Present:

_____
_____
_____
_____

Language Level 3 – Lesson 10

Exercise 2 — Day 47

Past:
_____
_____
_____

falls

Present:
_____
_____
_____

Past:
_____
_____
_____

(4) Which path will help the dog find the boy?

Name _____   Exercise **3** Day 48

Conjunctions

Conjunctions are words that join two words or phrases together. Here are some common conjunctions:

> and   but   or   nor   for   so

Study this example:

> Claire and Micah were thankful.

(1) Circle the conjunction in the sentence above.

Use the conjunctions above to complete the sentences. You may use each word more than once!

(2) I love pie, _____ I am full.

(3) You can either have apples _____ grapes.

(4) I would like apples _____ grapes.

(5) I want apples, _____ I like grapes, too.

(6) I do not like peaches, _____ do I like kiwi fruit.

(7) I put on my shoes _____ I could go outside.

Language Level 3 – Lesson 10

(8) Combine the two sentences using a conjunction.

My mom loves me very much.

My dad loves me very much.

Name _____   Exercise 4   Day 49

 **READING COMPREHENSION**

Read pages 28–29 of *101 Favorite Stories from the Bible* with your teacher.

Answer the questions on page 29.

Copy Hebrews 11:20, then memorize it with your teacher.

Copy the picture on page 29 and color it. Draw the whole picture or only the people. Copy the caption from page 29 below.

Language Level 3 – Lesson 10

Name_____   Exercise 5   Day 50

 **Words Ending in -ed and -ing**

We are going to work with words that have the suffix -ed and -ing.

Learn to spell these words:

> boasting, cried, dragged, hoping, hopping, pushed, saved, stopped, trying, using

Create your own word search with your spelling words.

- boasting
- cried
- dragged
- hoping
- hopping
- pushed
- saved
- stopped
- trying
- using

Write your spelling words on notecards. Write one word on each card. You may create right-brain flashcards with your words.

100   Language Level 3 – Lesson 10

# PICTURE STUDY

Lesson 11

Title: Ruth and Naomi parting from Orpah
Artist: Lifeway Collection

 **OBSERVATION SKILLS**

(1) Who are the three people in this picture?
(2) What is happening in this picture?
(3) What colors are used in this picture?
(4) How does this picture make you feel? Why?

Comprehension

The bear ran through the dark woods. The sun began to come up. The bear looked behind him.

Finish the story using at least two sentences.

_____
_____
_____
_____
_____
_____
_____
_____

Name _____   Exercise 2   Day 52

 **State of Being Verbs**

Some verbs show a state of being rather than an action. They link the subject to the predicate. Do you remember the 8 state of being verbs? If not, be sure to memorize them. They are:

is	are	were	been
am	was	be	being

Fill in the blank with the correct state of being verb for each sentence.

is   am   are

(1) He _____ a nice boy.

(2) I _____ late for work.

(3) We _____ going to church.

was   were

(4) Micah and Claire _____ thankful.

(5) Mr. Lopez _____ giving away Bibles.

Language Level 3 – Lesson 11   103

Exercise 2 — Day 52

be   been   being

(6) Ruth was _____ kind to Naomi.

(7) Ruth and Naomi have _____ on a long trip.

(8) They will _____ in Israel soon.

State of Being Word Search

(9) Find all eight state of being verbs in this word search. Words should be across and down only.

- am
- are
- be
- been
- being
- is
- was
- were

```
T C L L P U Z P J J
T Y B E E N J C N N
U W Y M X P Y B E G
Y B E I N G V Z W W
R N T G Q R H Z B R
W I S G I S B K A M
G A R E G Q J Z G Q
R B A N A W E R E X
F T A I V A O V R C
D M I L K S I Z Z B
```

Language Level 3 – Lesson 11

Compound Words

Compound words are made when we take two words and make them into one and create a new meaning. Here is an example:

$$\text{jelly + fish = jellyfish}$$

Use the pictures as clues and write the correct compound word.

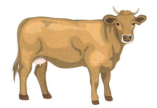  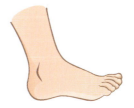 

(1) _____   (4) _____

  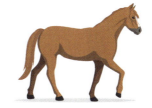 

(2) _____   (5) _____

(3) _____   (6) _____

Exercise 3 — Day 53

 Write a short story about this picture using as many compound words as you can.

Name_____ Exercise 4 Day 54

READING COMPREHENSION

Read pages 30–31 of *101 Favorite Stories from the Bible* with your teacher.

Answer the questions on page 31.

Copy Psalm 34:7, then memorize it with your teacher.

Copy the picture on page 31 and color it. Draw the whole picture or only the people. Copy the caption from page 31 below.

Language Level 3 – Lesson 11

Name _____   Exercise 5   Day 55

 **-oy and -oi Words**

We are going to work with -oy and -oi pattern words.

Learn to spell these words:

> avoid, choice, coil, destroy, enjoy, moist, oyster, poison, royal, voyage

Pretend you are writing in your journal. Tell about your day using all your spelling words if you can. You may use more than one spelling word in each sentence.

_____
_____
_____
_____
_____
_____
_____
_____
_____
_____
_____
_____

Circle the spelling words you used in your sentences.

Write your spelling words on notecards. Write one word on each card. You may create right-brain flashcards with your words.

108   Language Level 3 – Lesson 11

Lesson 12

A New Friend

There was an excited buzz in the classroom the next week as the students waited for Mr. Lopez. They were sharing their ideas after last week's lesson. One student said, "I am going to write a thank you letter to God!" Claire loved that idea and suggested they could put music to it and turn it into a praise song. Ava said, "Hey, maybe we could sing it at the Christmas play!" Micah was not at all excited about singing. Instead, he was planning to use his allowance to fill two shoeboxes for a child in another country. He had even started a shopping list!

As they were talking, Mr. Lopez walked in with a boy they didn't know. "Good morning! I want you all to meet Jin Lee. He and his family are visiting our church this morning."

Jin looked a little nervous, so Micah walked over and introduced himself. The rest of the students followed suit, and they soon discovered that Jin's family had just moved to town. The best part was that they moved into a house just two streets over from Micah! Before long, Jin was smiling. As the students took their seats, Mr. Lopez smiled to himself. He was happy to see his students being the "hands and feet of Jesus" as they welcomed a stranger. As he listened to their ideas, he explained that we have an opportunity to show gratitude to God in everything we do or think or say. Gratitude is an attitude! (Colossians 3:17)

(1) What were the children talking about while they waited for Mr. Lopez?

(2) Who did Mr. Lopez introduce?

(3) Why was Mr. Lopez happy?

(4) What did you learn from the story?

Name_____   Exercise 1   Day 56

Copywork

TEACHER NOTE • We have used the New American Standard version. You may assign the version your prefer.

"Whatever you do in word or deed, do all in the name of the Lord Jesus, giving thanks through Him to God the Father." Colossians 3:17

Copy the Scripture reference from the story.

_____
_____
_____
_____
_____
_____

Memorization

Memorize Colossians 3:17 with your teacher.

110 Language Level 3 – Lesson 12

Name_____   Exercise 2   Day 57

Adjectives

Adjectives describe a noun. Do you remember what a noun is? It is a person, place, or thing. An adjective describes a person, place, or thing.

An adjective can describe:

| color, size, shape | how many, looks, feels |
| tastes, smells, sounds | weather, feelings, behavior |

Circle the adjectives in the sentences that describe the color, size, or shape of a noun. Then underline the nouns.

(1) The gray cat jumped onto the large chair.

(2) The small, round balloon flew up into the blue sky.

Circle the adjectives in the sentences that describe how a noun tastes, smells, or sounds. Then underline the nouns.

(3) The sour candy is in the bowl.

(4) The loud thunder shook our house.

(5) The stinky skunk ran under the porch.

Write a sentence using at least one adjective that describes the color, size, or shape of a noun or how a noun tastes, smells, or sounds.

_____
_____
_____

Language Level 3 – Lesson 12

Exercise 2 — Day 57

Circle the adjectives in the sentences that describe how many, or how the noun looks or feels. Then underline the nouns.

(6) The five soft bunnies ran into the hole.

(7) The pretty bird sang two songs.

Circle the adjectives in the sentences that describe the weather, feelings, or behavior of a noun. Then underline the nouns.

(8) The rainy day kept the sad dog inside.

(9) The slow slug moved along the leaf.

Write a sentence using at least one adjective that describes how many, how a noun looks or feels, or that describes the weather, feelings, or behavior of a noun.

_____
_____
_____
_____

Language Level 3 – Lesson 12

Name_____ Exercise 3 Day 58

Contractions

Contract means to shrink or shorten. We create a contraction when we take two words, remove some letters, and make them into one word. We use an apostrophe where we took out letters. Study the example:

$$\text{you + have = you've}$$

Match the contractions to the words:

(1) could've   must have

(2) doesn't   I have

(3) wasn't   could have

(4) they'll   was not

(5) how's   does not

(6) I've   we would

(7) we'd   how is

(8) must've   they will

Write the correct contractions:

(9) did not _____   (15) do not _____

(10) they are _____   (16) has not _____

(11) you have _____   (17) you are _____

(12) let us _____   (18) I am _____

(13) we have _____   (19) will not _____

(14) are not _____   (20) is not _____

 Tell a story to your teacher about what might be happening in this picture. Use as many contractions as you can.

Name_____   Exercise 4   Day 59

 **READING COMPREHENSION**

Read pages 32–33 of *101 Favorite Stories from the Bible* with your teacher.

Answer the questions on page 33.

Copy Psalm 34:15, then memorize it with your teacher.

Copy the picture on page 33 and color it. Draw the whole picture or only the people. Copy the caption from page 33 below.

Language Level 3 – Lesson 12

Name _____ Exercise 5 Day 60

 **R-controlled Words**

We are going to work with -ar, -or, -er, ir, and -ur pattern words.

Learn to spell these words:

dirty, first, hurt, lunar, mayor, never, offer, rural, shirt, world

Unscramble each of the spelling words and write the word spelled correctly.

(1) trshi _____   (6) rnvee _____

(2) rrlau _____   (7) thru _____

(3) rlnau _____   (8) rmyao _____

(4) frfeo _____   (9) yrdti _____

(5) tsfri _____   (10) dlrwo _____

Write a fun sentence using at least two of your spelling words. Be sure to start your sentence with a capital letter and end it with a punctuation mark.

_____
_____
_____

Write your spelling words on notecards. Write one word on each card. You may create right-brain flashcards with your words.

Language Level 3 – Lesson 12

Lesson 13

Little Things
Dr. Ebenezer Cobham Brewer

Little drops of water,
Little grains of sand,
Make the mighty ocean
And the pleasant land.

Thus the little minutes,
Humble though they be,
Make the mighty ages
Of eternity.

Thus our little errors
Lead the soul away
From the path of virtue,
Far in sin to stray.

Little deeds of kindness,
Little words of love,
Make our earth an Eden,
Like the heaven above.

Little seeds of mercy,
Sown by youthful hands,
Grow to bless the nations
Far in heathen lands.

Comprehension
Were there any words you didn't understand? Circle them.

- The teacher should discuss with the student the meaning of the circled words in the context of the poem.

(1) What is the title of the poem?

(2) What is this poem about?

(3) Each section of the poem is called a stanza. There are five stanzas in this poem. Which stanza is your favorite? Why?

(4) How does this poem make you feel?

Written by Dr. Ebenezer Cobham Brewer in *One Thousand Poems For Children: A Choice Of The Best Verse Old And New*, edited by Roger Ingpen. Philadelphia: George W. Jacobs & Company Publishers, 1920. Page 50.

Name_____   Exercise 1   Day 61

Memorization

Memorize your favorite stanza of this poem with your teacher.

Rhyming

Write a rhyming word for each set of sentences.

(1) The cat ran up a tree.   _____
    She is high up but can still _____.

(2) I wonder what is in the box.   _____
    Could it be a pair of _____?

(3) I went swimming in a pool.   _____
    I was hot, but now I'm _____.

(4) "Read a book" my mom said.   _____
    So I took a book to read in _____.

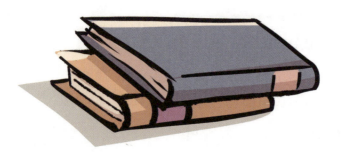

Language Level 3 – Lesson 13

Name_____ Exercise 2 Day 62

Adverbs

Adverbs are similar to adjectives, but instead of describing a noun, they tell about a verb.

An adverb often ends in -ly and describes *how*, *when*, *where*, or *how often* a verb happens. Study the example:

The dog barks loudly.

Do you see the adverb? The adverb is "loudly." It describes the verb "barks." It tells *how* the dog barks. Notice the adverb in this sentence ends with -ly.

An adverb can also tell when, where, or how often a verb happens. Study the examples:

I swam yesterday.

My dog walked outside.

I swim daily.

Do you see the adverb in each of the sentences?

In the first sentence, "yesterday" is an adverb that tells *when* I swam.

In the second sentence, "outside" is an adverb that tells *where* my dog walked.

In the third sentence, "daily" is the adverb tells *how often* I swim.

Language Level 3 – Lesson 13

Exercise 2 — Day 62

There are many adverbs. Here is a list of examples to study:

How	When	Where	How Often
gently	early	above	daily
quickly	now	inside	never
quietly	soon	here	often
sadly	tomorrow	outside	usually
safely	yesterday	upstairs	yearly

Fill in the blank of each sentence with an adverb:

The cat climbed the tree _____.

The girl sang _____.

The boy ran _____.

I can read _____.

Write a sentence using an adverb.

_____
_____
_____

Language Level 3 – Lesson 13

Quotation Marks

Quotation marks are used to show exactly what someone said.

Quotation marks at the beginning of a quote look like this: "

Quotation marks at the end of a quote look like this: "

Here is an example of a quote used in a sentence:

Mary said, "It is fun to read a poem."

Do you see the quotation marks? Show them to your teacher.

Practice putting quotation marks before and after this quote. Be sure to pay attention to the direction you make your marks. Show your quotation marks to your teacher after you write them:

__"Little seeds of mercy grow to bless the nations."__

- Please give students additional practice in the space below with writing quotation marks if needed. Some students may need the teacher to demonstrate writing quotation marks.

Add quotation marks to the sentences below. **Hint:** They go before and after a direct quote.

(1) Mom said, Use kind words with each other.

(2) Claire asked, How is showing mercy like planting seeds?

Language Level 3 – Lesson 13

Add quotation marks to the sentences below.

(3) Mr. Lopez explained, Small things can turn into big things.

(4) Micah yelled, Watch out for the car!

Did you notice there is a comma just before the quote starts? Circle the comma in each of the sentences above.

Did you notice the quote begins with a capital letter? Underline the capital letter at the beginning of each quote in the sentences above.

Write a sentence using a quote spoken by someone in your family. Start your sentence with the person's name.

- ○ Remember to use a comma before the quote.
- ○ Remember to use a capital letter to start the first word of the quote.
- ○ Remember to use quotation marks before and after the quote.

Name _____   Exercise 4   Day 64

 **READING COMPREHENSION**

Read pages 34–35 of *101 Favorite Stories from the Bible* with your teacher.

Answer the questions on page 35.

Copy James 3:16, then memorize it with your teacher.

_____
_____
_____
_____
_____
_____
_____

Copy the picture on page 35 and color it. You may draw the whole picture or only the people. Copy the caption from page 35 below.

_____
_____
_____
_____
_____
_____

Language Level 3 – Lesson 13

Name_____   Exercise 5   Day 65

 Plural Words

Learn to spell these words:

> begins, books, boxes, catches, horses,
> inches, keys, knees, pinches, tables

Fill in the correct spelling word for each sentence.

(1) My ruler measures in _____.

(2) Dad put his _____ on the table.

(3) The wood worker built two new _____.

(4) We packed many _____ when we moved.

(5) The book _____ with a sad story.

(6) They rode their _____ in the field.

(7) He got down on his _____ to pray.

(8) Ouch! This chair _____ me when I sit.

(9) Please take the _____ back to the library.

(10) The dog always _____ the ball.

Write your spelling words on notecards. Write one word on each card. You may create right-brain flashcards with your words.

CREATE YOUR OWN DICTIONARY!

124   Language Level 3 – Lesson 13

Lesson 14

Christmas Play Practice

The Christmas play was two weeks away, and Mrs. Pruitt had helped put the new praise song to music. She was playing the piano as some of the students practiced. Their song would be sung just before the play began. Mr. Lopez suggested they print out the words so the audience could sing along, so that week, the students designed a special song sheet and made enough copies to pass around.

Micah was so relieved this year when Jin volunteered to play one of the wise men. Micah had played that part for the last two years, when what he really wanted to do was run the sound system. This was his chance, and Pastor Pruitt had agreed he could train with one of the adults! It was a little complicated, but Micah took to it and learned quickly. He had never been so excited for the Christmas play!

After practice, they all enjoyed some homemade Christmas cookies. The annual cookie exchange had been on Saturday, so there were lots of yummy choices. Jin's mom even brought a tray of traditional Korean Christmas treats. They were crunchy ginger cookies coated with a sweet glaze and were undoubtedly Claire's favorite! Mr. Lee said it was a family recipe handed down from his grandmother who lived in South Korea. He had spent many Christmases with her and told them about some of the ways they celebrate the birth of Christ in that country. Play practice had turned into another lesson in the importance of celebrating the Lord.

(1) What would the children do before the Christmas play began?

(2) Why was Micah relieved?

(3) What did Jin's mom bring to practice?

(4) What lesson did the children learn at play practice?

Name_____   Exercise 1   Day 66

Write a Story

Write a short story about the picture using at least two or three sentences. You might even want to use a quote!

Hint: It may help to think about these things:

What is the duck doing? What is the elephant doing?

What other things are in the picture? Why do you think they are in the picture?

How do you think the duck feels? How do you think the elephant feels?

Prepositions

A preposition is a word that links a noun (or pronoun) to another word in the sentence. It shows a relationship between a noun and another word.

Prepositions show location. Study these common prepositions:

above	on	inside	in
below	off	outside	to
over	before	with	into
under	after	through	by

A *prepositional phrase* begins with a preposition and ends with a noun. Study the examples. The prepositional phrase is underlined:

Micah ran <u>outside of the house</u>.

Claire gave the ball <u>to the dog</u>.

In the first sentence, the preposition is *outside* and the noun is *house*.

In the second sentence, the preposition is *to* and the noun is *dog*.

In the sentences below, underline the prepositional phrase then circle the preposition.

(1) The bird flew through the window.

(2) Claire walked by the cat.

(3) Micah played with the dog.

(4) The ball went over the roof.

Exercise 2 Day 67

Write a sentence using a prepositional phrase. You may choose a preposition from one of the boxes on the previous page.

_____
_____
_____
_____

 JUST 4 FUN!

Describe as many positions of the bee to the flower as you can using prepositions.

Titles of Books, Movies, and Plays

When you write a sentence using the title of a book, movie, or play, you should:
- Underline the title (or use italics if you are using a computer)
- Capitalize the first and last word
- Capitalize all other words except small words that are not nouns, verbs, or adjectives such as: *the, for, and*

Study this example:

I read <u>The Big Book of History</u> in the fourth grade.

Underline the titles in the sentences below.

(1) <u>Passport to the World</u> is a fun book to read.

(2) I was in a play called <u>The Story of Ruth</u>.

(3) Have you watched <u>Extreme Caving</u> by Buddy Davis?

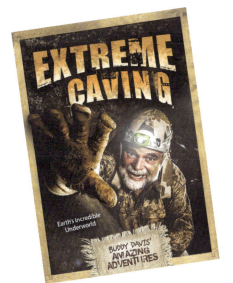

Language Level 3 – Lesson 14

Exercise 3 Day 68

Write the names of the book, movie, or play correctly.

(4) i dig dinosaurs

(5) whale of a story

(6) a special door

(7) pilgrim's progress

(8) the life of moses

Write a sentence using the title of a book, movie, or play.

Name_____   Exercise 4   Day 69

 **READING COMPREHENSION**

Read pages 36–37 of *101 Favorite Stories from the Bible* with your teacher.

Answer the questions on page 37.

Copy Psalm 128:1, then memorize it with your teacher.

_____
_____
_____
_____
_____
_____
_____

Copy the picture on page 37 and color it. Draw the whole picture or only the people. Copy the caption from page 37 below.

_____
_____
_____
_____
_____
_____
_____

Language Level 3 – Lesson 14

Name_____ Exercise 5 Day 70

Plural Words

We are going to work with plural words that change the f to v and y to i.

Learn to spell these words:

> babies, copies, families, flies, knives,
> leaves, loaves, ladies, shelves, thieves

Write a funny story using as many spelling words as you can in each sentence.

_____
_____
_____
_____
_____
_____
_____
_____
_____
_____
_____
_____
_____

Circle the spelling words in your sentences.

Write your spelling words on notecards. Write one word on each card. You may create right-brain flashcards with your words.

Language Level 3 – Lesson 14

 **PICTURE STUDY**

Lesson 15

Title: The Snowstorm (Winter) (1786-1787)

Artist: Francisco de Goya

 **OBSERVATION SKILLS**

Observation

(1) In what season does this painting take place?

(2) What things do you see in the picture?

(3) What is happening in this painting?

(4) Describe the people in this painting.

(5) What colors are used in this picture?

(6) How does this picture make you feel? Why?

Language Level 3 – Lesson 15

Name_____   Exercise 1   Day 71

Story Writing

Finish this story about the picture using at least two or three sentences:

It was a cold, hard winter. The travelers were tired, but they had to keep going. The wind was blowing hard, and the sun had set.

Name _____ Exercise 2 Day 72

 **Homophones: To – Too – Two**

Copy the sentence about homophones:

Homophones are words that sound the same but have different meanings.

_____
_____
_____
_____

The words *to, too,* and *two* all sound the same, but they have different meanings.

- to = direction   too = also or a lot   two = number

Circle the homophones *to, too*, and *two* in the silly sentence:

(1) My family and I went to two parks with our two friends before we went to two zoos to see too many zebras to count and an elephant, too.

Language Level 3 – Lesson 15   135

Exercise 2 — Day 72

Write a sentence using: to

Write a sentence using: too

Write a sentence using: two

 Just 4 Fun!

Tell your teacher a story about this picture using the words: to, too, and two.

Name_____   Exercise 3   Day 73

Dictionary Guide Words

TEACHER NOTE
- The student will need a dictionary for this lesson. A children's dictionary is recommended. Also, students may need to review alphabetizing before completing this lesson.

Ask your teacher for a dictionary. Open the dictionary to any page. You will see two words at the top of the page, usually one on each side. These are called *guide words*. They tell you the first and last words that are found on the page.

Here is an example of guide words:

| feline   ferry |

Now, look at the words with definitions listed on the page of your dictionary. They are in alphabetical order. The first word is the first guide word. The last word is the last guide word.

In our example, words listed on the page in alphabetical order could include: *fell, felt, fence, fern*. They are after *feline* but before *ferry*.

Guide words make it easier to look up words in the dictionary.

Open your dictionary to any page. Write the guide words:
_____   _____
_____   _____

Write any two words found on the page in alphabetical order:
_____   _____
_____   _____

Language Level 3 – Lesson 15

Exercise 3 — Day 73

Put the following words under the correct guide words:

duck   door   dove   dust   drain   dune

donut　　　　　draw	dry　　　　　dye
(1) _____	(4) _____
(2) _____	(5) _____
(3) _____	(6) _____

Ask your teacher to help you look up these words in your dictionary:
- ant
- moon
- snail

Name_____ Exercise 4 Day 74

READING COMPREHENSION

Read pages 38–39 of *101 Favorite Stories from the Bible* with your teacher.

Answer the questions on page 39.

Copy John 15:12, then memorize it with your teacher.

Copy the picture on page 39 and color it. Draw the whole picture or only the people. Copy the caption from page 39 below.

Language Level 3 – Lesson 15

Name _____ Exercise 5 Day 75

 **Irregular Plural Words**

We are going to work with irregular plural words.

Learn to spell these words:

> cacti, children, corn, deer, fish,
> geese, mice, people, sheep, women

Find the spelling words in the word search.

- ○ cacti
- ○ children
- ○ corn
- ○ deer
- ○ fish
- ○ geese
- ○ mice
- ○ people
- ○ sheep
- ○ women

```
Y C H I L D R E N I P M
D E E R F K O V W P C J
C J I R Y B A P T M A W
O R A G Y S R E P A C O
R R N S Z N P O G X T M
N D X R W G U P E M I E
Q M I R Q U Q L E I M N
Y O K J C Y W E S C E Z
K Q X B K Z F K E E S X
T S H E E P Q Q F I S H
```

Write your spelling words on notecards. Write one word on each card. You may create right-brain flashcards with your words.

140 Language Level 3 – Lesson 15

Lesson 16

God's Gift

As they practiced and performed the Christmas play over the past several years, Mrs. Pruitt was thankful to be the director. She loved helping the students learn and act out the true meaning of Christmas. They began to understand that the ultimate Christmas gift was not a new bicycle or video game, but that God had given the gift of Himself. He became a man so that people could know Him.

A few weeks ago, as play practice began, Mrs. Pruitt asked the students to imagine what life would be like without God. This assignment made Claire's friend, Ava, think. In many ways, it had been a hard year for her family. Her Mom had been sick and in the hospital twice. Her brother had broken his leg, which meant extra chores for her. Then, to top it off, one of her good friends had moved to another town! But she had learned to talk to God about everything, and most nights, they prayed together as a family. She looked forward to when her Mom or Dad would read to them from the Bible, and they would talk about the stories. She realized they were not so different from the people mentioned in the Bible. She needed God in her life.

Mrs. Pruitt had gotten Ava to realize how thankful she was for God's gift. It made such a difference to know God cared about everything. This year as she performed, she prayed that everyone who was watching the play could know how much God cared about them, too.

(1) What is the true meaning of Christmas?
(2) Who is Ava?
(3) Why did Ava's family have a hard year?
(4) What did Ava learn from going through such difficulties?
(5) How does the story end?

Name _____ Exercise 1 Day 76

Word Categories

The nouns, verbs, and adjectives have gotten all mixed up! Put them under the correct column.

> run cat sweet pretty ball tree yell fast jump

Nouns   **Verbs**   **Adjectives**

(1) _____   (4) _____   (7) _____

(2) _____   (5) _____   (8) _____

(3) _____   (6) _____   (9) _____

Short Story

Write a short story using some of the nouns, verbs, and adjectives above.

_____
_____
_____
_____
_____
_____
_____
_____

Name_____   Exercise 2   Day 77

 **There – Their – They're**

Do you remember what homophones are? They are words that sound the same but mean something different.

The words *there*, *their*, and *they're* all sound the same, but they have different meanings.

> there = a place
> their = belonging to others
> they're = a contraction that means "they are"

Circle *there*, *their*, and *they're* in the following sentences:

(1) They're going on a field trip.

(2) I love their garden.

(3) The cat ran over there.

Write a sentence using: there
_____
_____

Write a sentence using: their
_____
_____

Write a sentence using: they're
_____
_____

Language Level 3 – Lesson 16

Name_____   Exercise **3**   Day 78

Sentences

A sentence must express a complete thought. Cross out each line that is not a sentence:

(1) She has green.   (3) Name is Polly.

(2) I love my parrot.   (4) She eats seeds.

Do you remember the four types of sentences? They are:

Imperative: This type of sentence is a command.
Declarative: This type of sentence is a statement.
Exclamatory: This type of sentence is an exclamation and has emotion.
Interrogative: This is a big word that means a question.

What kind of sentences are these?

Put an **IM** for Imperative, **D** for Declarative, **E** for Exclamatory, and **IN** for Interrogative:

(5) ____ What is the true meaning of Christmas?

(6) ____ Jesus came to the earth as a baby.

(7) ____ Don't fall off the stage!

(8) ____ Go get the song list.

Underline the subject of each sentence. Circle the predicate in each sentence.

(9) Jin and Ava practiced for the play.

(10) Ava and her family prayed and read the Bible.

Language Level 3 – Lesson 16

Name_____   Exercise 4   Day 79

 **READING COMPREHENSION**

Read pages 40–41 of *101 Favorite Stories from the Bible* with your teacher.

Answer the questions on page 41.

Copy Hebrews 11:24-25, then memorize it with your teacher.

Copy the picture on page 41 and color it. Draw the whole picture or only the people. Copy the caption from page 41 below.

Language Level 3 – Lesson 16

Name_____   Exercise 5   Day 80

Compound Words

We are going to work with compound words.

Learn to spell these words:

> airplane, anything, bookcase, breakfast, everyone, hallway, inside, keyboard, rainbow, sunshine

Write silly sentences until you have used all the spelling words. Put as many words as you can into each sentence.

_____
_____
_____
_____
_____
_____
_____
_____
_____
_____
_____

Circle each of the spelling words in your sentences.

Write your spelling words on notecards. Write one word on each card. You may create right-brain flashcards with your words.

Language Level 3 – Lesson 16

 **Lesson 17**

Psalm 23

The LORD is my shepherd,
I shall not want.
² He makes me lie down in green pastures;
He leads me beside quiet waters.
³ He restores my soul;
He guides me in the paths of righteousness
For His name's sake.
⁴ Even though I walk through the valley of the shadow of death,
I fear no evil, for You are with me;
Your rod and Your staff, they comfort me.
⁵ You prepare a table before me in the presence of my enemies;
You have anointed my head with oil;
My cup overflows.
⁶ Surely goodness and lovingkindness will follow me all the days of my life,
And I will dwell in the house of the LORD forever.

Comprehension

Were there any words you didn't understand? Circle those words.

- The teacher should discuss with the student the meaning of the circled words in the context of the psalm.

(1) What chapter of Psalms did you read?

(2) How many verses are there in this chapter?

(3) Do you remember what a psalm is?

(4) What is this psalm about?

(5) What did you learn about God in this psalm?

(6) What were your favorite verses?

Name _____ Exercise 1 Day 81

Memorization

Memorize with your teacher the first three verses of this psalm. Can you memorize all six verses?

Matching

Match the first part of each verse with the second part:

(1) The Lord is my shepherd,　　He leads me beside quiet waters.

(2) He makes me lie down in green pastures;　　He guides me in the paths of righteousness For His name's sake.

(3) He restores my soul;　　I shall not want.

(4) Even though I walk through the valley of the shadow of death,　　And I will dwell in the house of the Lord forever.

(5) You prepare a table before me in the presence of my enemies;　　You have anointed my head with oil; My cup overflows.

(6) Surely goodness and lovingkindness will follow me all the days of my life,　　I fear no evil, for You are with me; Your rod and Your staff, they comfort me.

Language Level 3 – Lesson 17

Name_____   Exercise 2   Day 82

 **Articles**

An *article* comes before a noun. There are three articles: *a, an, the*

We use the word *a* before words that start with a consonant. Here is an example:

Claire read a psalm.

We use the word *an* before words that start with a vowel. Here is an example:

Micah ate an apple.

| a + consonant | an + vowel |

We use *a* and *an* to refer to any noun.

We use *the* when we refer to a specific noun. Here is an example:

Ava read a book.
Ava read the Bible.

Write *a, an,* or *the* correctly in the sentences.

(1) Jin was in _____ Christmas play at church.

(2) Micah gave _____ cookie to Ava.

(3) Claire put on _____ apron.

Language Level 3 – Lesson 17

Exercise 2 — Day 82

Write a sentence using the article: a

Write a sentence using the article: an

Write a sentence using the article: the

Making Lemonade!

Create a poster for a lemonade stand. Be sure to include the price for each glass and at least one sentence that describes the lemonade!

Name_____   Exercise 3   Day 83

Paragraphs

A *paragraph* is a group of sentences about a specific idea or topic. A paragraph should:

- Start on a new line with an indent.
- Include at least four sentences.
- Start with a topic sentence.
- Include 2–3 sentences that give details about the topic.
- End with a concluding sentence. It ends the paragraph by saying the topic in another way.

Here is an example:

INDENT   **TOPIC SENTENCE**

   Ava and Jin are friends. They met at church. They like to sit with each other in Sunday school. They like to play four square after church. Ava and Jin are glad they met!

DETAIL SENTENCES

CONCLUDING SENTENCE

Writing a paragraph is like making a sandwich. You use a piece of bread for the top and bottom with the good stuff in between.

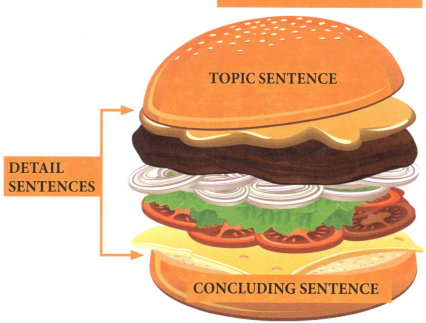

Language Level 3 – Lesson 17

Exercise 3 — **Day 83**

Write a paragraph about something you like. It can be about a pet, favorite food, or something you like to do, like riding your bike. Check off each part as you write your paragraph:

- ○ Write the topic sentence. Remember to indent your topic sentence.
- ○ Write 2-3 sentences that give details about your topic. (**Hint:** Some things you like about your pet, favorite food, or activity.)
- ○ Write a concluding sentence.

_____
_____
_____
_____
_____
_____
_____
_____
_____
_____

Did you use a capital letter to start each sentence? Did you use correct punctuation at the end of each sentence? Good job!

Name _____   Exercise 4   Day 84

READING COMPREHENSION

Read pages 42–43 of *101 Favorite Stories from the Bible* with your teacher.

Answer the questions on page 43.

Copy Jeremiah 1:7b-8, then memorize it with your teacher.

Copy the picture on page 43 and color it. Draw the whole picture or only the people. Copy the caption from page 43 below.

Language Level 3 – Lesson 17

Exercise 5 — Day 85

 **Spelling Practice**

Contractions

We are going to work with contractions.

Learn how to spell these words:

> can't, he's, I'm, it'll, let's,
> she'd, they're, we've, won't, you're

Write the contraction for each set of words.

(1) they are _____   (6) it will _____

(2) he is _____   (7) she would _____

(3) you are _____   (8) I am _____

(4) can not _____   (9) let us _____

(5) we have _____   (10) will not _____

Write a fun sentence using at least two of your spelling words. Be sure to start your sentence with a capital letter and end it with a punctuation mark.

_____
_____
_____

Write your spelling words on notecards. Write one word on each card. You may create right-brain flashcards with your words.

Language Level 3 – Lesson 17

Lesson 18

A Celebration

Today was December 31. Mr. Lopez thought it would be fun to have a celebration today since New Year's Eve fell on a Sunday this year. He had asked the students to think back over the special feast days they had studied and plan a special celebration. They would invite all the other Sunday school classes for one BIG feast in the auditorium!

There was excitement in the air as Mr. Lopez started the feast by blowing the shofar. Then the Sunday school students led everyone in a prayer of thanksgiving. Micah's and Jin's fathers had agreed to cook pancakes and sausage while some of the other parents pitched in with the remaining items for the feast. All the students from the class helped serve the food.

Before the celebration began, Claire and Ava had put paper and pens on each table along with instructions for everyone to make a list of some things they were thankful for during the last year. While they were eating, many people stood and shared their list with everyone. There were many smiles and lots of applause as they listened to all the blessings of God. Pastor Pruitt stood and remarked how good it is to remember and share these things, and he quoted Psalm 105:1, "Oh give thanks to the Lord; call upon His name; make known His deeds among the peoples!" Then he suggested they make this feast an annual event at the church!

With full hearts and bellies, everyone headed to the morning worship service.

(1) What idea did Mr. Lopez have?

(2) What are some things they did at the celebration?

(3) What is Psalm 105:1 about?

(4) What are some things you are thankful for?

Memorization

Memorize Psalm 105:1 with your teacher.

 OBSERVATION SKILLS

A *fact* is something that is true.

An *opinion* is how someone feels about something. It may or may not be true.

Study the picture. Write **F** for fact or **O** for opinion next to each sentence about the picture.

(1) ____ It is snowing.

(2) ____ The birds are hungry.

(3) ____ The birds are sitting on a branch.

(4) ____ The birds want to fly south.

Name _____   Exercise 2   Day 87

2nd Quarter Review
(Each question is 4 points)

TEACHER NOTE • Give student access to the Study Sheets in the back of the book while completing this Review.

Action Verbs

Circle the verb in each sentence. Tell whether the verb is in the present or past tense.

(1) Claire runs to class. _____ tense

(2) Claire ran to class. _____ tense

Fill in the blank with the correct state of being verb for each sentence.

is   am   are

(3) He _____ a nice boy.

(4) I _____ late for work.

(5) We _____ going to church.

was   were

(6) Micah and Claire _____ thankful.

(7) Mr. Lopez _____ giving away Bibles.

Language Level 3 – Lesson 18

Exercise 2 — Day 87

> be   been   being

(8) Ruth was _____ kind to Naomi.

(9) Ruth and Naomi have _____ on a long trip.

(10) They will _____ in Israel soon.

Circle the adjectives in the sentences. Then underline the nouns.

(11) The stinky skunk ran under the porch.

(12) The slow slug moved along the leaf.

Underline the adverbs in the sentences.

(13) The cat climbed the tree quickly.

(14) The girl sang a song yesterday.

In the sentences below, underline the prepositional phrase then circle the preposition.

(15) Claire walked by the cat.

(16) The ball went over the roof.

Exercise 2 — Day 87

Match the words with the correct meaning.

(17) to   number
(18) too   also or a lot
(19) two   direction

Match the words with the correct meaning.

(20) there   belonging to others
(21) their   they are
(22) they're   a place

Write a, an, or the correctly in the sentences.

(23) Jin was in _____ Christmas play at church.

(24) Micah gave _____ cookie to Ava.

(25) Claire put on _____ apron.

Language Level 3 – Lesson 18

Name_____ Exercise 3 Day 88

2nd Quarter Review
(Each question is 4 points)

TEACHER NOTE • Give student access to the Study Sheets in the back of the book while completing this Review.

Circle the conjunctions in the sentences.

(1) I love pie, but I am full.

(2) You can have apples and grapes.

Match the words to create a compound word:

(3) tooth   boy
(4) cow   ball
(5) foot   brush

Write the correct contractions:

(6) did not _____   (7) they are _____

Add quotation marks to the sentence below.

(8) Mom said, Use kind words with each other.

Underline the title in the sentence below.

(9) Passport to the World is a fun book to read.

Put the following words under the correct guide words:

duck   door

donut draw	dry dye
(10) _____	(11) _____

Language Level 3 – Lesson 18

Exercise 3 Day 88

A sentence must express a complete thought. Cross out each line that is not a sentence:

(12) I love my parrot. (13) Name is Polly.

Underline the subject of each sentence. Circle the predicate sentence.

(14) Jin and Ava practiced for the play.

(15) Ava and her family prayed and read the Bible.

The sentences are mixed up! Help us fix the paragraph by matching them to the correct part of the paragraph.

(16) A paragraph is like a sandwich. — First Detail Sentence

(17) You start with a sentence, which is the first piece of bread. — Topic Sentence

(18) You add detail sentences for the meat, cheese, and mustard. — Concluding Sentence

(19) Then you write an ending sentence for the bottom piece of bread. — Third Detail Sentence

(20) I like to make paragraph sandwiches! — Second Detail Sentence

Language Level 3 – Lesson 18

Exercise 3 — Day 88

Put an **IM** for Imperative, **D** for Declarative, **E** for Exclamatory and **IN** for Interrogative:

(21) ____ What is the true meaning of Christmas?

(22) ____ Jesus came to the earth as a baby.

(23) ____ Don't fall off the stage!

(24) ____ Go get the song list.

(25) Write a paragraph about a place you like to go.

Check off each part as you write your paragraph:

○ Write the topic sentence. Remember to indent your topic sentence.

○ Write 2-3 sentences that give details about your topic. (**Hint:** Some things you like about your pet, favorite food, or activity.)

○ Write a concluding sentence.

Name_____   Exercise 4   Day 89

READING COMPREHENSION

Read pages 44–45 of *101 Favorite Stories from the Bible* with your teacher.

Answer the questions on page 45.

Copy Psalm 140:12, then memorize it with your teacher.

Copy the picture on page 45 and color it. Draw the whole picture or only the people. Copy the caption from page 45 below.

Language Level 3 – Lesson 18

Name_____   Exercise 5   Day 90

 **Spelling Review**

Use your flashcards to practice your spelling words.

You may:
- Ask someone to quiz you on how to spell the words
- Play spelling games found in the back of the book
- Create your own spelling games
- Use each word in a sentence and say them to your teacher

Students may choose their own spelling words this week for their dictionary. They may add their words to the spelling words section in the back of the book.

 **Add it up!**

Each letter has a number with it. Add up the combined number for each of the following words:

(1) play _____

(2) lazy _____

(3) church _____

(4) cookies _____

(5) singing _____

(6) Christmas _____

(7) Which words have the smallest number? Write them here: _____ _____

164   Language Level 3 – Lesson 18

Lesson 19

A New Winter Challenge

"We are going to begin the new year with another Bible memory challenge," Mr. Lopez said. "Just like last year, there will be a special prize for all students who successfully complete the challenge. This year, we will memorize Philippians 4:4–5 and Colossians 3:12–15."

Micah remembered how scared he was when they started the challenge last year, but now he knew he could do it! Last year, he and Claire had worked together for weeks until they had it done. They memorized all thirteen verses from 1 Corinthians, chapter 13! He looked across the room and noticed the expression on Jin's face. He looked just like Micah must have last year — scared! So, Micah asked Jin if he would like to be his partner for the challenge. "You can do this, Jin. You just need to memorize one or two verses each week. We will do it together!"

Claire was just about to ask Micah to be her partner when she heard their conversation. She had just assumed that she and Micah would pair up again. They had worked so well together before, and they were best friends. At least, she thought they were. Claire tried to hide her disappointment and walked over to the other students as Mr. Lopez was passing out the verses.

"Does anyone need a partner?" Claire asked. Ava grabbed her hand and said, "I do! I was hoping we could pair up this year! We will make a great team!" Claire smiled, but she could not help feeling a little sad at the same time.

(1) What was the challenge given by Mr. Lopez?

(2) Why did Micah ask Jin to be his partner?

(3) How did Claire feel about this?

Memorization

Mr. Lopez' class is going to memorize Philippians 4:4–9 and Colossians 3:12–15. We can too! Work with your teacher over the next two weeks to memorize Philippians 4:4–5.

Write a Story

Write a paragraph about the picture.

Check off each part as you write your paragraph:

- ○ Write the topic sentence. Remember to indent your topic sentence.
- ○ Write 2-3 sentences that give details about your story. (**Hint:** Think about how the boy and the dog feel about each other. Are they having fun?)
- ○ Write a concluding sentence.

Name_____ Exercise 2 Day 92

 **Has – Have – Had**

The verbs *has* and *have* show there is possession.

Possession means something belongs to someone.

We use the words *I, you, they*, or *we* with the helping verb *have*.

We use the words *he, she,* or *it* with the helping verb *has*.

have		has	
I have	they have	he has	she has
you have	we have	it has	

Study the examples of *have* and *has*:

They <u>have</u> a Bible.

He <u>has</u> a Bible.

When we are talking about something in the past, we use the word *had*.

Study the examples of *had*:

I <u>had</u> a Bible.

Fill in the correct verb *has* or *have* in the sentences.

(1) He _____ a cute dog.

(2) They _____ fun playing catch.

Language Level 3 – Lesson 19   167

Exercise 2 — Day 92

Write a sentence using the verb: has

Write a sentence using the verb: have

Write a sentence using the verb: had

Help the girl and her dog get out of the maze.

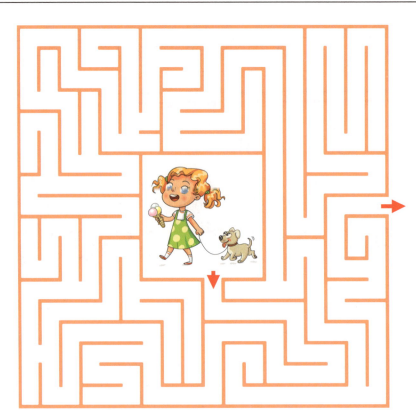

Name_____   Exercise 3   Day 93

Sentence Combining

We can make our writing better by combining sentences. Study the example:

The cow was in the field. The cow was eating grass.

We can combine these two sentences into one.

The cow was in the field eating grass.

Combine the following sentences into one sentence.

(1) Claire waved at Ava. Claire waved at Micah.

_____
_____
_____

Combine the following sentences into one sentence.

(2) Micah ran to Claire. Micah ran quickly.

_____
_____
_____

Combine the following sentences into one sentence.

(3) Ava met Jin. Claire met Jin.

_____
_____
_____

Language Level 3 – Lesson 19

Exercise 3 Day 93

The sentences are mixed up! Help us fix the paragraph by matching them to the correct part of the paragraph.

(4) A paragraph is like a sandwich. — First Detail Sentence

(5) You start with a sentence, which is the first piece of bread. — Topic Sentence

(6) You add detail sentences for the meat, cheese, and mustard. — Concluding Sentence

(7) Then you write an ending sentence for the bottom piece of bread. — Third Detail Sentence

(8) I like to make paragraph sandwiches! — Second Detail Sentence

Name _____   Exercise 4   Day 94

 **READING COMPREHENSION**

Read pages 46–47 of *101 Favorite Stories from the Bible* with your teacher.

Answer the questions on page 47.

Copy Ecclesiastes 8:11, then memorize it with your teacher.

Copy the picture on page 47 and color it. Draw the whole picture or only the people. Copy the caption from page 47 below.

Language Level 3 – Lesson 19

Name_____ Exercise 5 Day 95

 **-r Words**

We are going to work with -air, -are, -oar, -ore, and -ure pattern words.

Learn to spell these words:

> before, board, care, cure, dairy, future, hair, mare, shore, soar

Write the spelling words in the correct boxes. **Note:** Some words have the same shape!

(1)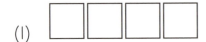

(2)

(3)

(4)

(5)

(6)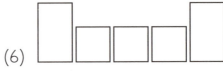

(7)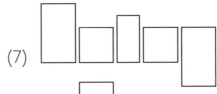

(8)

(9)

(10)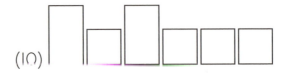

Write your spelling words on notecards. Write one word on each card. You may create right-brain flashcards with your words.

Language Level 3 – Lesson 19

 PICTURE STUDY

Lesson 20

Title: David and Goliath

Artist: Bill Looney

 OBSERVATION SKILLS

(1) Who are the people in the picture?

(2) What is happening in the picture?

(3) What colors are used in the picture?

(4) How does this picture make you feel? Why?

Language Level 3 – Lesson 20

Name_____ Exercise 1 Day 96

Rhyming

Write two sentences that end with a rhyme. You may use any rhyming words, but here are some ideas:

look : book   saw : law   sad : glad

_____
_____
_____

Write two more sentences that rhyme.

_____
_____
_____

Find these 15 objects in the picture.

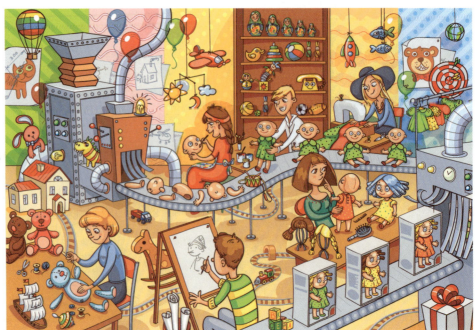

Language Level 3 – Lesson 20

Name_____   Exercise 2   Day 97

 **Has — Have — Had**

Last week, we studied how to use the verbs *has*, *have*, and *had*. These verbs can also be used as *helping verbs*.

Helping verbs help the main verb in a sentence.

Look for helping verbs *before* the main verb in a sentence.

We are going to work with the helping verbs: *has, have, had*

Study the examples:

Jin <u>has worked</u> on his verse.

Jin and Micah <u>have worked</u> together.

Claire <u>had felt</u> sad.

The helping verb and the main verb are underlined in each sentence.

We use *has* when the noun in the subject is singular. (Singular means one.)

In the first sentence, Jin is a singular noun.

We use *have* when the there is more than one noun in the subject.

In the second sentence, Jin and Micah are two people. The subject is plural. (Plural means more than one.)

We use *had* when the action happened in the past. This is called past tense. The third sentence shows that in some time in the past, Claire felt sad.

Remember:

Single	Plural	Past Tense
has	have	had

Language Level 3 – Lesson 20

Exercise 2 Day 97

Fill in the blank with the correct verb: has have

(1) Claire and Ava _____ brushed the cat.

(2) Jin _____ walked the dog.

Write a sentence using the helping verb: had

_____
_____
_____

Be a Star!

Be nice and become a light in someone's life today. Make a difference by just being you! Help others and be a star. Say or do something nice for your mom or dad, sister or brother. Take a moment and tell someone "thank you!" Share a smile. Tell a nice joke. (Or pick up stuff off the floor in your room!)

You are a star!

Language Level 3 – Lesson 20

Name_____   Exercise 3   Day 98

Synonyms, Antonyms, Thesaurus

> Synonyms are two words that mean the same thing.

Copy the sentence about synonyms.

_____
_____
_____
_____

Here are some examples of synonyms:

fast : quick   large : big   stop : pause

- Can you think of some synonyms? Say them to your teacher.

> Antonyms are two words that have opposite meanings.

Copy the sentence about antonyms.

_____
_____
_____
_____

Here are some examples of antonyms:

fast : slow   large : small   stop : go

- Can you think of some antonyms? Say them to your teacher.

Exercise 3 — Day 98

Match the synonyms!

(1)	close	glad
(2)	happy	jog
(3)	give	near
(4)	rest	pass
(5)	run	relax

Match the antonyms!

(6)	open	sad
(7)	happy	shut
(8)	give	work
(9)	rest	walk
(10)	run	take

A *thesaurus* is a book of synonyms and antonyms. We can use a thesaurus to help us find the best words to use in our writing.

TEACHER NOTE • We suggest using a children's thesaurus for this activity.

Do you remember how to look up words in a dictionary? Finding words in the thesaurus is done the same way. Instead of giving you the definition of a word, a thesaurus gives you synonyms and antonyms of a word.

Ask your teacher for a thesaurus. Find in the thesaurus the word: add

Write a synonym and an antonym for the word: add

_____   _____

Spend some time with your teacher looking at words in the thesaurus. Be sure to read the word and the synonyms and antonyms for that word. You may want to think of a sentence using the word you are going to look up and say it to your teacher. Say the sentence again, but use a synonym of the word. Then say it using an antonym. Have fun!

You may have noticed that not all words have antonyms listed. Why do you think that is? Talk about this with your teacher.

Name_____   Exercise 4   Day 99

 **READING COMPREHENSION**

Read pages 48–49 of *101 Favorite Stories from the Bible* with your teacher.

Answer the questions on page 49.

Copy I Corinthians 5:7b, then memorize it with your teacher.

_____
_____
_____
_____
_____
_____

Copy the picture on page 49 and color it. Draw the whole picture or only the people. Copy the caption from page 49 below.

_____
_____
_____
_____
_____
_____

Language Level 3 – Lesson 20

Name _____ Exercise 5 Day 100

 **SPELLING PRACTICE** Learn to spell these words:

> play, plow, press, prison, shape,
> shingle, shut, thank, that, then

Solve the riddles using the spelling words.

(1) The opposite of open. _____

(2) How to be grateful. _____

(3) A place you do not want to be. _____

(4) Something kids like to do. _____

(5) The outline of something. _____

(6) A farmer does this to a field. _____

(7) Found on the top of a house. _____

(8) Not this but _____.

(9) First this, _____ that.

(10) To push down on something. _____

Write your spelling words on notecards. Write one word on each card. You may create right-brain flashcards with your words.

 CREATE YOUR OWN DICTIONARY!

 **Lesson 21**

Do Not be Anxious About Anything

As soon as Claire arrived at church on Wednesday night, she noticed Micah and Jin talking in the hallway. They were making plans to spend the day together on Saturday. Jin's dad was going to take them to the skate park in the morning, and then they were going to practice their verses in the afternoon. Micah was so involved in the conversation, he didn't even say "Hi!" as she walked over to them. She was just about to say something herself when Ava ran over and asked her if she wanted to practice together before church began.

Ava had learned last year that it was helpful to write the verses by hand and had already done that several times since Sunday. She had half of the Philippians passage memorized!

As Claire listened to Ava, the words "Do not be anxious about anything" touched her. This was exactly how she was feeling. She was anxious about her friendship with Micah. And when she realized how much Ava had memorized, she started to feel anxious about the challenge as well. She had not even looked at the verses!

Claire planned to study that evening. She read over the verses but was struggling to memorize them. She knew what she needed to do and found a quiet spot on the back porch to pray. She asked God to help her have a thankful heart, to not feel anxious or jealous of Micah and Jin's friendship, and to help her have the peace those verses talked about.

(1) Where does the story take place?
(2) What were Micah and Jin's plans for Saturday?
(3) Why was Claire anxious?
(4) What helped Claire?

Memorization

Mr. Lopez's class is working to memorize Philippians 4:4–9 and Colossians 3:12–15. We can, too! Work with your teacher over the next two weeks to memorize Philippians 4:6–7.

Reading the Map!

Now that you are learning more about maps, it is important to know how to read one. See if you can answer the following questions for your teacher:

(1) Is the market or the gas station closer to the hospital?

(2) Is the gymnasium or the circus located in the center of town?

(3) Is the hot air balloon on the north or south part of the map?

(4) Is the gymnasium closer to the tire center or the circus?

Name_____   Exercise 2   Day 102

 **See — Saw — Seen**

We are going to work with some more verbs: *see*, *saw*, *seen*.

| I see. | I saw. | I have seen. |

The verbs *see* and *saw* are used alone.

The verb *see* refers to the present.

The verb *saw* refers to the past.

The verb *seen* refers to the past and needs a helper verb. Do you remember what a helping verb is? A helping verb helps the main verb in a sentence.

Study the examples:

I see Micah in class.

I saw him with Jin.

I have seen Claire in class, too.

Fill in the blank with the correct verb: **see saw seen**

(1) I have _____ Micah and Jin work on their memory verse.

(2) I _____ Ava write down her Bible verse yesterday.

(3) I _____ Claire every Sunday.

Language Level 3 – Lesson 21   183

Exercise 2 — Day 102

Write a sentence using: see
_____

Write a sentence using: saw
_____

Write a sentence using: seen
_____

Use the words "*see, saw, seen*" to fill in the blanks about this picture. Use each word only once.

(4) I _____ two children reading to animals in the forest. Can you _____ them too? I have never _____ anything like it!

Language Level 3 – Lesson 21

Name_____   Exercise 3   Day 103

Homophones and Homonyms

> Homophones are two words that sound the same.
> Homophones have different meanings.
> They are not spelled the same.

Study the example of homophones:

> I can see it is raining outside.
> The waves from the sea wash up shells.

> Homonyms are two words that sound the same.
> Homonyms have different meanings.
> They are spelled the same.

Study the example of homonyms:

> The boy set the block on the tower.
> The clouds will block the sun.

Remember:

Homophones	Homonyms
· sound the same · different meanings · spelled differently	· sound the same · different meanings · spelled the same
Example: male — mail	Example: glasses — glasses

Language Level 3 – Lesson 21

Exercise 3   Day 103

Match homophones and homonyms to each correct description. **Hint:** Each word has more than one answer.

(1) homophones
(2) homonyms

sound the same
different meaning
same spelling
different spelling

Choose from the homophones to write two sentences.

blue : blew   buy : bye   cell : sell

_____
_____
_____
_____

Choose from the homonyms to write two sentences. Remember to use a different meaning for each homonym. You may ask your teacher for help if you aren't sure of the two meanings.

bat : bat   bark : bark   palm : palm

_____
_____
_____
_____

Language Level 3 – Lesson 21

Name_____ Exercise 4 Day 104

READING COMPREHENSION

Read pages 50–51 of *101 Favorite Stories from the Bible* with your teacher.

Answer the questions on page 51.

Copy Hebrews 11:29, then memorize it with your teacher.

Copy the picture on page 51 and color it. Draw the whole picture or only the people. Copy the caption from page 51 below.

Language Level 3 – Lesson 21

Name_____   Exercise **5**   Day 105

 **Blends**

We are going to work with blends.

Learn to spell these words:

> brick, camp, check, inspect, loft,
> mend, mold, pond, pump, swift

Create your own word search with your spelling words.

- brick
- camp
- check
- inspect
- loft
- mend
- mold
- pond
- pump
- swift

Write your spelling words on notecards. Write one word on each card. You may create right-brain flashcards with your words.

Language Level 3 – Lesson 21

Lesson 22

The New Book
By Mrs. Elisabeth Turner

A neat little book, full of pictures, was bought
For a good little girl that was glad to be taught.
She read all the tales, and then said to her mother,
"I'll lend this new book to my dear little brother.
He shall look at the pictures and find O and I,
I'm sure he won't tear it, he's such a good boy!
Oh, no! brother Henry knows better indeed,
Although he's too young, yet, to spell or to read."

Comprehension
Were there any words you didn't understand? Circle them.

- The teacher should discuss with the student the meaning of the circled words in the context of the poem.

(1) What is the title of the poem?
(2) Who wrote this poem?
(3) What is this poem about?
(4) How does this poem make you feel? Why?

Mrs. Elisabeth Turner in *One Thousand Poems For Children: A Choice Of The Best Verse Old And New*, edited by Roger Ingpen. Philadelphia: George W. Jacobs & Company Publishers, 1920. Page 97.

Name _____   Exercise 1   Day 106

Memorization

Memorize at least four lines of this poem.

TEACHER NOTE • Both the teacher and the student should work together to memorize the stanza.

Rhyming

Write a rhyming word for each set of sentences.

(1) Whenever I am feeling down, _____
My big brown dog comes _____.

(2) He likes to go outside to run. _____
I throw him a ball. It's lots of _____.

(3) He lays by my bed as I go to sleep. _____
I whisper to him as I count some _____.

(4) My dog is a very good friend.
Each day is so fun, I don't like it to _____

Language Level 3 – Lesson 22

Name_____   Exercise 2   Day 107

 **Eat — Ate — Eaten, Go — Went — Gone**

We are going to work with some more verbs: *eat*, *ate*, *eaten* and *go*, *went*, *gone*

| I eat. | I ate. | I have eaten. |
| I go. | I went. | I have gone. |

The verbs *eat* and *go* refer to the present.

    I eat lunch at noon.

    I go swimming in our pool.

The verbs *ate* and *went* refer to the past.

    I ate a banana for a snack.

    I went for a swim last night.

The verbs *eaten* and *gone* refer to the past and need a helping verb.

    I have eaten my dinner.

    I have gone swimming every day.

Draw a line from the sentence to the correct verb:

(1)   I have _____ lunch already.   eat

(2)   I _____ my last banana earlier.   eaten

(3)   I _____ dinner every day.   ate

Exercise 2 — Day 107

Write a sentence using: go

Write a sentence using: went

Write a sentence using: gone

 Tell your teacher a story about this picture using the words go, went, and gone.

Language Level 3 – Lesson 22

Prefix: un-, re-

A *prefix* is letters added to the beginning of a word to change the meaning. We can add the prefix *un-* and *re-* to a word.

The prefix un- means not.
The prefix re- means again.

Here is an example:

load: unload, reload

What does the word *load* mean? Tell your teacher.
What does the word *unload* mean? Tell your teacher.
What does word *reload* mean? Tell your teacher.

Add the prefix *un-* to each word.

(1) do: _____

(2) fair: _____

Add the prefix *re-* to each word.

(3) move: _____

(4) turn: _____

Exercise 3 — Day 108

Write a sentence using words with the prefix *un-* and *re-*. Here is an example:

> Micah thought it was unfair that he had to redo his homework.

JUST 4 FUN!

Complete the dot to dot, then color it.

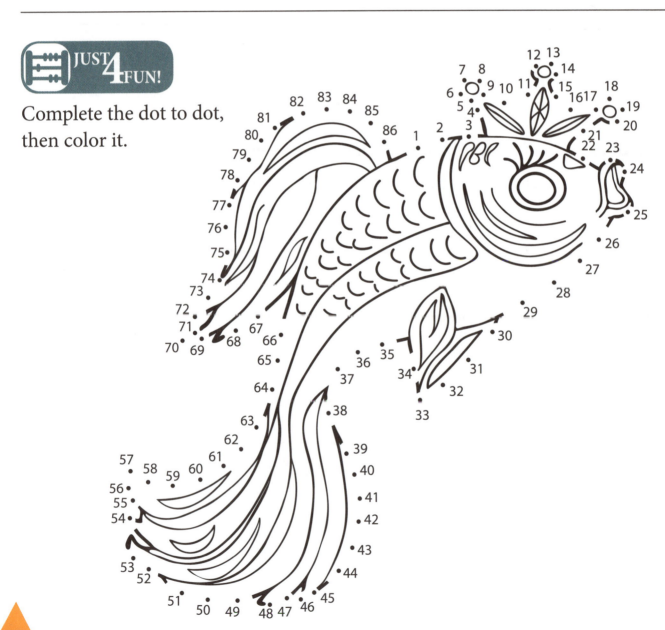

194 Language Level 3 – Lesson 22

Name _____   Exercise 4   Day 109

READING COMPREHENSION

Read pages 52–53 of *101 Favorite Stories from the Bible* with your teacher.

Answer the questions on page 53.

Copy Psalm 78:25, then memorize it with your teacher.

_____
_____
_____
_____
_____
_____
_____

Copy the picture on page 53 and color it. Draw the whole picture or only the people. Copy the caption from page 53 below.

_____
_____
_____
_____
_____
_____

Language Level 3 – Lesson 22

Name _____ Exercise 5 Day 110

 **Homophones**

Learn to spell these homophones:

> meat, meet, knows, nose, pair,
> pear, peace, piece, stair, stare

Fill in the blanks with homophones to complete the silly sentences.

(1) My _____ _____ a stinky skunk.

(2) The _____ sat on a _____ of plates.

(3) We will _____ to eat _____.

(4) Before I step on the _____, I will _____ at it to make sure I don't trip.

(5) I have _____ about the _____ of pie that fell off my plate.

Write your spelling words on notecards. Write one word on each card. You may create right-brain flashcards with your words.

196 Language Level 3 – Lesson 22

Lesson 23

The Lord is Near

Claire felt so much better after praying. The words from Philippians began to make sense to her in a fresh way. "The Lord is near" means that God already knows everything going on in our lives and that He hears our prayers. Just knowing that alone brings a feeling of peace!

As Claire sat there, Patch came over and began to rub back and forth against her legs as if to say, "Hey, I missed you." He jumped into Claire's lap and lay himself down right smack on top of her memory verses. Claire laughed and gently pulled her verses out from under him and began to study them again. Memorizing was definitely more interesting with a fluffy little ball of fur purring in your lap.

Ava called the next day to see if Claire wanted to practice over the weekend. She said she would be at the community center on Saturday for her big brother's basketball tournament and wondered if Claire could come. Ava's mom could even pick her up. Claire's parents agreed, so the girls spent Saturday practicing their verses between ballgames, hot dogs, popcorn, and a game or two of foursquare with some of the other kids who were there. Claire had the best time, and by the end of the day, they had both finished memorizing all of the Philippians passage and were starting on Colossians!

(1) What made Claire feel peace?

(2) What did Patch do?

(3) How did Ava and Claire spend their Saturday?

Name_____   Exercise 1   Day 111

Memorization

Mr. Lopez's class is working to memorize Philippians 4:4–9 and Colossians 3:12–15. We can, too! Work with your teacher over the next two weeks to memorize Philippians 4:8–9.

Writing a Story

Let's write a story about the panda.

Look at the picture. Circle the sentence that is the best topic sentence.

(1) The panda jumped up and down.

(2) The panda ate bamboo.

(3) The panda was old.

(4) The panda laid down at the end of a long day.

Exercise 1 Day 111

Circle the best group of sentences that give details about the topic sentence about the panda.

(5) She ran through the woods. She ate grapes. She swam in the river.

(6) They fished before they ate lunch.

(7) He thought about the fun he had that day. He surprised his mom with flowers he picked himself. Then he swam with his brother and sister all day.

(8) The panda didn't like to eat bamboo. He liked to eat apples. He ate lettuce instead.

Circle the sentence that is the best ending sentence for the story.

(9) The panda ran through the house as fast as he could.

(10) The panda was tired but happy.

(11) The panda went out and fixed the car.

(12) The panda made an apple pie.

● Read to your teacher the topic sentence, detail sentences, and ending sentences you circled to create a story. Does your story make sense? If it doesn't, talk with your teacher about which sentences would make a better story.

Language Level 3 – Lesson 23

Name_____   Exercise 2   Day 112

 **Most – Almost**

We are going to work with the words *most* and *almost*.

| most = the largest amount | almost = nearly |

Study the examples:

I have the most cherries in my bowl.
I am almost done eating them.

Fill in the correct word:

| most   almost |

(1) I _____ finished my lunch.

(2) I have the _____ to eat.

Write a sentence using: most
_____
_____

Write a sentence using: almost
_____
_____

Language Level 3 – Lesson 23

Exercise 2 — Day 112

Sit – Set

Now we are going to work with the words *sit* and *set*.

sit = rest in an upright position

set = place an object

Study the examples:

I like to sit outside in my lawn chair.
I set my books on the desk.

Fill in the correct word:

sit   set

(3) I _____ at the table.

(4) I _____ my cup on the table.

Write a sentence using: sit
_____
_____

Write a sentence using: set
_____
_____

Language Level 3 – Lesson 23

Exercise 2 Day 112

Go — Went — Gone

We are going to work with some new verbs: *go, went, gone*.

| I go. | I went. | I have gone. |

The verbs *go* and *went* can be used alone.

The verb *go* refers to the present.

The verb *went* refers to the past.

The verb *gone* refers to the past and needs a helping verb. Study the examples:

I go to bed each night.
I went to bed early last night.
I have gone to bed late most nights.

Fill in the blank with the correct verb:

go   went   gone

(5) I have _____ to that playground many times.

(6) I _____ to the store yesterday.

(7) I _____ get the mail every day.

Name _____ Exercise 3 Day 113

Prefix: in-, im-, dis-, pre-, tele-

A *prefix* is letters added to the beginning of a word to change the meaning. We learned that we can add the prefix *un-* and *re-* to a word. There are many more prefixes we can add to words. We can add:

in-   im-   dis-   pre-   tele-

Study the meanings of the prefixes:

> in- means not, in, or on
> im- means not, in, or on
> (use im- for words that begin with b, m, and p)
> dis- means not or opposite of
> pre- means before
> tele- means far or distant

Here is an example:

prove: disprove

What does the word *prove* mean? Tell your teacher.

What does word *disprove* mean? Tell your teacher.

Add the prefix *im-* to the word.

(1) port: _____

Add the prefix *in-* to the word.

(2) take: _____

Language Level 3 – Lesson 23

Exercise 3 — Day 113

Add the prefix *dis-* to each word.

(3) like: _____

(4) trust: _____

Add the prefix *pre-* to each word.

(5) test: _____

(6) made: _____

Add the prefix *tele-* to each word.

(7) phone: _____

(8) vision: _____

Tell your teacher what each word means.

Name_____   Exercise 4   Day 114

 **READING COMPREHENSION**

Read pages 54–55 of *101 Favorite Stories from the Bible* with your teacher.

Answer the questions on page 55.

Copy James 4:12a, then memorize it with your teacher.

Copy the picture on page 55 and color it. Draw the whole picture or only the people. Copy the caption from page 55 below.

Language Level 3 – Lesson 23

Name_____ Exercise 5 Day 115

 **Homonyms**

We are going to work with homonyms.

Learn to spell these words:

> can, duck, fly, leaves, light, match, pitcher, ring, ruler, yard

Word scramble

Unscramble each of the spelling words and write the word spelled correctly.

(1) hmtca _____   (6) grni _____

(2) dyra _____   (7) rrleu _____

(3) vsleea _____   (8) rphtcei _____

(4) tlhgi _____   (9) kdcu _____

(5) yfl _____   (10) nca _____

Pick a spelling word. Write a silly sentence using the word twice but with a different meaning each time.

_____
_____
_____

Write your spelling words on notecards. Write one word on each card. You may create right-brain flashcards with your words.

Language Level 3 – Lesson 23

 PICTURE STUDY

Lesson 24

Title: Summer and Playing Children (1913)

Artist: Nikolai Astrup

 OBSERVATION SKILLS

(1) In what season do you think this painting takes place?

(2) What things do you see in the picture?

(3) What is happening in this painting?

(4) Describe the people in this painting.

(5) What colors are used in this picture?

(6) How does this picture make you feel? Why?

Language Level 3 – Lesson 24

Story Writing

Finish this story about the picture.

It was time for lunch but dad was still working hard in the field.

_____
_____
_____
_____
_____
_____

Can you think of a different story for the picture? How would it start? Tell the story to your teacher.

Name_____   Exercise 2   Day 117

 **This – That – These – Those**

We use the words *this* and *that* when we are talking about one of something. We call this singular.

We use the word *this* if the object is close to the person speaking.

We use the word *that* if the object is far away.

We use the words *these* and *those* when we are talking about more than one of something. We call this plural.

We use the word *these* if the objects are close to the person speaking.

We use the word *those* if the objects are far away.

	Near	Far
Singular	this	that
Plural	these	those

Fill in the blank with the correct word:

that   those

(1) I want _____ book.

(2) _____ are my pencils.

Write a sentence using: this

_____
_____

Write a sentence using: these

_____
_____

Language Level 3 – Lesson 24   209

Name _____ Exercise 3 Day 118

Suffix: -ed, -ing

A *suffix* is letters added to the end of a word to change the meaning. We can add the suffix *-ed* and *-ing* to a word. Here is an example:

> jump: jumped, jumping

If the word ends with a silent e, then we drop the e before adding the suffix. Here is an example:

> race: raced, racing

Add the suffix *-ed* and *-ing* to the word.

(1) bake: _____ _____

When we have a word with one syllable, one short vowel, and it ends with one consonant, we must double the consonant then add -ed or -ing.

Pop has one syllable, one short vowel, and it ends with one consonant. We must double the *p* before we add -ed or -ing. Here is an example:

> pop: popped, popping

Add the suffix *-ed* and *-ing* to the word.

(2) stop: _____ _____

Remember these examples:

> jump : jumped, jumping
> race : raced, racing
>   silent e = drop the e
>
> pop : popped, popping
>   one syllable, one short vowel, ends in one consonant = double the consonant

Language Level 3 – Lesson 24

Exercise 3 Day 118

Follow the rules you learned to add the suffix -ed and -ing to each word.

(3) add: _____ _____

(4) taste: _____ _____

(5) rip: _____ _____

Root Words

We added the suffix -ed and -ing to words. We also added prefixes to words. The words we add a suffix or a prefix to is called a *root word*. Here is an example:

We can add the suffix -ed to the word *walk* to make a new word:

walked

walk is the *root word*. -ed is the suffix.

We can add the prefix re- to the word *move* to make a new word:

remove

move is the *root word*. Re- is the prefix.

Circle the root word:

(6) wished

(7) undone

(8) resell

(9) playing

Language Level 3 – Lesson 24

Name _____ Exercise 4 Day 119

Read pages 56–57 of *101 Favorite Stories from the Bible* with your teacher.

Answer the questions on page 57.

Copy I Corinthians 10:7, then memorize it with your teacher.

Copy the picture on page 57 and color it. Draw the whole picture or only the people. Copy the caption from page 57 below.

Language Level 3 – Lesson 24

Exercise 5 — Day 120

Words with a Prefix

We are going to work with words that have the prefix dis-, im-, in-, re-, and un-.

Learn to spell these words:

> discover, dislike, immature, impolite, inactive, intake, reheat, return, undone, unpack

Find the spelling words in the word search.

- discover
- dislike
- immature
- impolite
- inactive
- intake
- reheat
- return
- undone
- unpack

```
N F Z Z F Q N T K E A N
G U D I S L I K E C B R
D N B J N C O N O N F I
I P X W D I N T A K E M
Z A O C R E T U R N R P
L C P E R E H E A T A O
L K I N A C T I V E S L
H D D I S C O V E R N I
I I M M A T U R E W G T
H B O U N D O N E L E E
```

Language Level 3 – Lesson 24

Exercise 5 Day 120

Write a fun sentence using at least two of your spelling words. Be sure to start your sentence with a capital letter and end it with a punctuation mark.

_____
_____
_____
_____

Write your spelling words on notecards. Write one word on each card. You may create right-brain flashcards with your words.

Optional Activities

• If student needs more practice, you may assign these additional activities.

Write your spelling words.

(1) _____   (6) _____

(2) _____   (7) _____

(3) _____   (8) _____

(4) _____   (9) _____

(5) _____   (10) _____

Ask your teacher to read each spelling word. Spell the word out loud to your teacher and use it in a sentence.

214   Language Level 3 – Lesson 24

 **Lesson 25**

A Distraction

Jin and Micah were starving after their lively skateboard race at the skate park. Mr. Lee asked them if they wanted burgers and fries or pizza. Both sounded good, so they decided to flip a coin. And the winner was . . . – burgers and fries!

They arrived at Jin's house with full bellies and a plan to start working on their memory verses. Micah had his verses in hand when he walked into Jin's room, but what he saw there took his mind in another direction completely. He had never seen so many LEGOs™ in one place! Jin had several completed projects on a bookshelf and had even built the LEGO™ City Police Command Center! He also had a LEGO™ building table organized with drawers and shelves full of blocks and building plans. Without another thought of memory verses, the boys began to plan their next build.

When Jin's mom checked in to see how they were coming along, she found them knee-deep in LEGO™ bulldozers and helicopters. "I think you'd better come to the dining room table to work on your verses," she said.

Micah felt bad as they finally started to practice. He had promised to help Jin and instead had gotten caught up in having fun. He remembered how much it had helped him last year when Claire encouraged him, and this year's challenge was only three weeks away! They really needed to buckle down if they were going to get these verses memorized on time.

(1) How did Jin and Micah decide on what to eat?

(2) What caused Jin and Micah to be distracted?

(3) Why did Jin's mom suggest they move to the dining room table?

(4) Why did Micah feel bad?

Name_____   Exercise 1   Day 121

Memorization

Mr. Lopez's class is working to memorize Philippians 4:4–9 and Colossians 3:12–15. We can, too! Work with your teacher over the next two weeks to memorize Colossians 3:12–13.

Truth or Fiction

Read the story:

> There was a fox who could fly to the top of the highest tree. Every morning, he would fly up and sit at the top of a very tall pine tree. He would watch all of the animals in the forest. He would then fly down and startle them. The animals wished the fox didn't know how to fly.

Truth means something that is true or real.

Fiction is a story that is made up or not true.

(1) Is this story based on truth or fiction?
_____
_____

(2) What clue helped you to know this?
_____
_____
_____
_____

Name_____ Exercise 2 Day 122

 **It's – Its, Who's – Whose**

The word *it's* is a contraction. Do you remember what a contraction is? A contraction is two words that are shortened into one. The word *it's* is a contraction of *it is*. Here is an example:

> It's time to work on our verses.

Read the sentence again and see if you could say "it is" instead of "it's." This is an easy way to see if a contraction is being used.

In Lesson 8, we learned that a possessive noun shows who or what owns or has something. We make a singular noun possessive by adding an apostrophe and an "s." However, there are exceptions. Exceptions are when the rules are broken. An exception means we need to pay close attention and remember it. We are about to learn about an exception, so pay close attention.

The word **its** means possession or belonging, but we don't use an apostrophe in this case. It is an exception to the rule. Here is an example:

> The cat hurt its leg.

The word *its* shows that the leg that is hurt belongs to the cat. Notice we didn't use an apostrophe and an "s" to show possession. Only the contraction of *it is* uses the apostrophe.

Remember:

| it's = it is | | its = possession (and breaks the rules) |

Write the correct word in the sentences: it's   its

(1) The dog buried _____ bone.

(2) _____ sunny outside.

Language Level 3 – Lesson 25

Exercise 2 — Day 122

The word *who's* is a contraction that means *who is*. Here is an example:

Who's going to the skate park today?

Read the sentence again and see if you could say "who is" instead of "who's." In the sentence above, you can replace "who's" with "who is" so we know it is a contraction and needs an apostrophe.

The word *whose* is a pronoun. It is a possessive form of *who*. Here is an example:

Whose skateboard is this?

Did you notice that *whose* also breaks the rules? It shows possession but doesn't use an apostrophe. Only the contraction of *who is* uses the apostrophe.

Remember:

| who's = who is | | whose = possession (and breaks the rules) |

Write the correct word in the sentences: who's whose

(3) _____ coming to the picnic?

(4) _____ dog is this?

Whose Balloon is Whose?

(5) Trace the strings of each balloon to see which child is holding it. Color the correct balloon color under each child.

Name_____ Exercise **3** Day 123

Simile

> A simile compares two different things using the words like or as.

Hint: The word *simile* is close to the word *similar*. Similar means almost the same.

Here is an example of the two types of similes. The first sentence uses the simile *as*. The second sentence uses the simile *like*:

Jin and Micah built a tower as tall as a tree.

Jin and Micah are like two peas in a pod.

We call a simile a *figure of speech*. We say this because the tower isn't really as tall as a tree. We are saying it is really tall by comparing the tower to a tree. In the same way, Jin and Micah aren't really peas, are they? They are just close friends and like to do similar things.

We can make our sentences fun by using similes.

Finish the sentences using a simile. You may use more than one word:

My dog barks as loud as _____.

I can jump as high as _____.

My brother runs like _____.

Thanksgiving dinner smells like _____
_____.

Language Level 3 – Lesson 25

219

Exercise 3 Day 123

Write a sentence using the simile: as

_____
- -
_____
- -
_____

Write a sentence using the simile: like

_____
- -
_____
- -
_____

 Use the words *like* or *as* to describe as many objects as possible in this image.

Language Level 3 – Lesson 25

Name _____   Exercise 4   Day 124

 **READING COMPREHENSION**

Read pages 58–59 of *101 Favorite Stories from the Bible* with your teacher.

Answer the questions on page 59.

Copy Psalm 33:18, then memorize it with your teacher.

_____
_____
_____
_____
_____
_____

Copy the picture on page 59 and color it. Draw the whole picture or only the people. Copy the caption from page 59 below.

_____
_____
_____
_____
_____

Language Level 3 – Lesson 25   221

Name _____ Exercise 5 Day 125

 **Words with a Suffix**

We are going to work with words that have the suffix -est, -ied, -less, -ly, and -y.

Learn to spell these words:

> biggest, carried, closest, copied, directly, endless, finally, healthy, thirsty, useless

Write silly sentences until you have used all the spelling words. Put as many words as you can into each sentence.

_____
_____
_____
_____
_____
_____
_____
_____
_____
_____

Circle each of the spelling words in your sentences.

Write your spelling words on notecards. Write one word on each card. You may create right-brain flashcards with your words.

 READING TOGETHER

Psalm 47

O clap your hands, all peoples;
Shout to God with the voice of joy.
² For the Lord Most High is to be feared,
A great King over all the earth.
³ He subdues peoples under us
And nations under our feet.
⁴ He chooses our inheritance for us,
The glory of Jacob whom He loves. Selah.

⁵ God has ascended with a shout,
The Lord, with the sound of a trumpet.
⁶ Sing praises to God, sing praises;
Sing praises to our King, sing praises.
⁷ For God is the King of all the earth;
Sing praises with a skillful psalm.
⁸ God reigns over the nations,
God sits on His holy throne.
⁹ The princes of the people have assembled themselves as the people of the God of Abraham,
For the shields of the earth belong to God;
He is highly exalted.

Comprehension

Were there any words you didn't understand? Circle these words.

 TEACHER NOTE
- The teacher should discuss with the student the meaning of the circled words in the context of the psalm.

Name _____ Exercise 1 Day 126

NARRATION PRACTICE

(1) What chapter of Psalms did you read?

(2) Did you pause and think at the Selah?

(3) How many verses are there in this chapter?

(4) What is this psalm about?

(5) What did you learn about God in this psalm?

(6) What were your favorite verses?

Memorization

Memorize with your teacher at least two verses of this poem. The verses should be in a row and may be picked by you or your teacher.

Write a Psalm

Work with your teacher to write a short psalm. It should have at least two verses. Remember, a psalm is a song. It praises God. After you write your psalm, think of a tune and sing it!

Name_____   Exercise 2   Day 127

 **Comparison using -er and -est**

Using a simile is one way we can compare two things. Another way is to use the suffixes -er and -est.

Adding -er to a word shows that there is more of something than another. Here is an example:

> I am taller than my brother.

We added the suffix -er to the word *tall* to show I have more height than my brother.

Adding -est to a word shows that there is the most of something. Here is an example:

> I am the tallest in my family.

We added the suffix -est to the word *tall* to show I have the most height in my family.

> If a word ends in an e, we remove the e before we add the suffix -er or -est.

Here is an example:

> My cat is nicer than a lion.
>
> My cat is the nicest cat I know.

We added -er and -est to the word *nice*. We dropped the "e" before adding our suffix.

Language Level 3 – Lesson 26   225

Exercise 2 — Day 127

Add the suffix *-er* and *-est* to the following words:

(1) fast: _____   _____

(2) slow: _____   _____

(3) tame: _____   _____

Write a sentence using the suffix: −er
_____
_____

Write a sentence using the suffix: −est
_____
_____

Connect and color!

Draw a line to connect the dots starting at number 1. When you have connected all the dots, pick your favorite colors to color in the pretty picture. When you complete your coloring, see if you can tell your teacher a story about it, using some -er and -est words!

226   Language Level 3 – Lesson 26

Name _____ Exercise 3 Day 128

Writing a Paragraph

Do you remember what a paragraph is? A paragraph is a group of sentences about a specific idea or topic.

Remember, a paragraph should:

- Start on a new line with an indent.
- Include at least four sentences.
- Start with a topic sentence.
- Include 2-3 sentences that give details about the topic.
- End with a concluding sentence. This sentence ends the paragraph by saying the topic in another way.

Do you remember our paragraph sandwich? You use a piece of bread for the top and bottom with the good stuff in between.

Write a paragraph about something you are good at. It can be about a school subject, sport, special talent like singing or art, or something you can do fast. It can be something you have practiced a lot or something that comes easy to you. It can even be something like being nice to your sister!

Here is an example of a paragraph I wrote about something that I am good at:

I am good at making scrapbooks. I like to arrange pictures of my family on a big piece of paper. I add lots of colorful stickers to make my pages fun. Sometimes I add ribbon, colorful tape, and glitter to my pages. When my scrapbook is done, my family loves to look at our fun memories.

Language Level 3 – Lesson 26

Exercise 3 — **Day 128**

Check off each part as you write your paragraph:
- ○ Write the topic sentence. Remember to indent your topic sentence.
- ○ Write 2-3 sentences that give details about your topic. (**Hint:** Tell why you are good at it. You may also tell how you do what you are good at.)
- ○ Write a concluding sentence.

_____
_____
_____
_____
_____
_____
_____
_____
_____
_____
_____
_____

Did you use a capital letter to start each sentence? Did you use correct punctuation at the end of each sentence? Good job!

Language Level 3 – Lesson 26

Name_____   Exercise 4   Day 129

 **READING COMPREHENSION**

Read pages 60–61 of *101 Favorite Stories from the Bible* with your teacher.

Answer the questions on page 61.

Copy Psalm 18:30, then memorize it with your teacher.

Copy the picture on page 61 and color it. Draw the whole picture or only the people. Copy the caption from page 61 below.

Language Level 3 – Lesson 26

Name_____ Exercise 5 Day 130

SPELLING PRACTICE

Roots

We are going to work with the roots *bio*, *graph*, *phon*, and *scope*.

Learn to spell these words:

autograph, biography, biology, biopsy, graph, microscope, phone, photograph, scope, symphony

Write the spelling words in the correct boxes.

(1) photo☐☐☐☐

(2) sym☐☐☐☐☐

(3) ☐☐☐☐☐scope

(4) bio☐☐☐☐☐☐

(5) auto☐☐☐☐☐

(6) ☐☐☐☐

(7) bio☐☐

(8) ☐☐☐☐☐

(9) bio☐☐☐☐

(10) ☐☐☐☐☐

Write your spelling words on notecards. Write one word on each card. You may create right-brain flashcards with your words.

CREATE YOUR OWN DICTIONARY!

Language Level 3 – Lesson 26

Lesson 27

The Peace of Christ

The next morning after Sunday School, Micah confided in Claire that he and Jin were behind on their verses. He told her she had been such a good friend and helped him so much last year that he wanted to do the same for Jin because he was really nervous about the challenge.

Claire was relieved to know the reason Micah had chosen Jin to be his partner. She and Micah were still friends! She told him that she had gotten behind on her verses also, but that she had worked really hard and was on schedule now. "We still have three weeks until the challenge. You can do this, Micah," she said. Then she told him Ava's idea to write the verses down. Micah thought that was smart and planned to share the idea with Jin. Claire was right; if they worked hard for the next three weeks, they could do it.

"Thanks, Claire. I'm thankful to have a friend like you!" Micah said. "And I know you and Ava will do great on the challenge."

Over the next three weeks, everyone worked hard, especially Micah and Jin, but when the challenge arrived, they were all ready.

As Mr. Lopez passed out prizes, Claire realized that this year's challenge had taught her some valuable lessons. She thought of the last verse in their Colossians passage: *"Let the peace of Christ rule in your hearts, to which indeed you were called in one body; and be thankful."* Now that was a prize worth keeping!

(1) What did Micah confide to Claire?

(2) Why was Claire relieved?

(3) What idea did Claire share with Micah?

(4) What lessons do you think Claire learned from the memory verse challenge?

Name _____ Exercise 1 Day 131

Memorization

Mr. Lopez's class is working to memorize Philippians 4:4–9 and Colossians 3:12–15. We can, too! Work with your teacher over the next two weeks to memorize Colossians 3:13–15.

Classifying

You are going on a trip and taking four suitcases with you. Fill each suitcase with related words from the list. Check off each word once you put it in a suitcase.

- ○ socks
- ○ apple
- ○ ball
- ○ Bible
- ○ game
- ○ atlas
- ○ crackers
- ○ shirt
- ○ dictionary
- ○ blocks
- ○ pants
- ○ carrot
- ○ cheese
- ○ hat
- ○ thesaurus
- ○ teddy bear

(1) Clothes

(3) Food

(2) Books

(4) Toys

Language Level 3 – Lesson 27

Name_____   Exercise 2   Day 132

3rd Quarter Review
(Each question is 4 points)

• Give student access to the Study Sheets in the back of the book while completing this Review.

Match the correct verb.

(1) Micah and Jin ____ said their verses.   has
(2) Claire ____ written a poem.   have
(3) I have ____ the Lord's mercy.   see
(4) I ____ Micah help Jin last week.   seen
(5) I can ____ Ava reading her Bible.   saw
(6) I will ____ my lunch soon.   eaten
(7) I have ____ my snack already.   ate
(8) I ____ my breakfast early this morning.   eat
(9) I will ____ to bed soon.   went
(10) I have ____ to bed early every night.   go
(11) I ____ to bed late last night.   gone
(12) I am ____ done reading my book.   most
(13) I have ____ of my room clean.   almost
(14) ____ your book on the table.   Sit
(15) ____ down and tell me about your day.   Set

Language Level 3 – Lesson 27

Exercise 2   Day 132

(16) I want ____ Bible to read.   these

(17) Do ____ look like my socks?   that

(18) I like ____ apples.   this

(19) Is ____ my pencil?   those

(20) The cat lost ____ toy.   it's

(21) Mom, ____ going to rain soon.   its

(22) ____ coming to our house after church?   Whose

(23) ____ Bible is this?   Who's

Add the suffix *-er* and *-est* to the following words:

(24) fast: _____   _____

(25) white: _____ _____

Language Level 3 – Lesson 27

Name_____ Exercise 3 Day 133

3rd Quarter Review
(Each question is 5 points)

TEACHER NOTE
- Give student access to the Study Sheets in the back of the book while completing this Review.

Combine the following sentences into one sentence.

(1) Jin studied the verses. Micah studied the verses.

_____
_____
_____
_____

Match the synonyms!   Match the antonyms!

(2) close   glad   (5) open   take
(3) happy   pass   (6) happy   shut
(4) give   near   (7) give   sad

Match homophones and homonyms to each correct description. (**Hint:** Each word has more than one answer.)

(8) homophones   sound the same
(9) homonyms   different meaning
                   same spelling
                   different spelling

Follow the rules you learned to add the suffix *-ed* and *-ing* to each word.

(10) add: _____ _____

(11) taste: _____ _____

(12) rip: _____ _____

Language Level 3 – Lesson 27

235

Exercise 3 **Day 133**

Circle the root word, then underline the prefix:

(13) un<u>less</u>   (15) re<u>move</u>   (17) in<u>come</u>

(14) dis<u>trust</u>   (16) pre<u>made</u>   (18) tele<u>phone</u>

Finish the sentences using a simile. You may use more than one word:

(19) The skunk smells as bad as a _____.

(20) The cat runs like _____.

Bonus: (10 points)

Write a paragraph about your favorite color. Be sure to tell why you like it. You may also want to tell about some things that have that color.

Check off each part as you write your paragraph:

○ Write the topic sentence. Remember to indent your topic sentence. (2 points)

○ Write 2-3 sentences that give details about your topic. (6 points)

○ Write a concluding sentence. (2 points)

_____
_____
_____
_____
_____
_____

Did you use a capital letter to start each sentence? Did you use correct punctuation at the end of each sentence? Good job!

Language Level 3 – Lesson 27

Name_____   Exercise 4   Day 134

READING COMPREHENSION

Read pages 62–63 of *101 Favorite Stories from the Bible* with your teacher.

Answer the questions on page 63.

Copy John 3:14-15, then memorize it with your teacher.

Copy the picture on page 63 and color it. Draw the whole picture or only the people. Copy the caption from page 63 below.

Language Level 3 – Lesson 27

Name_____   Exercise 5   Day 135

 **Spelling Review**

Use your flashcards to practice your spelling words.

You may:

- Ask someone to quiz you on how to spell the words
- Play spelling games found in the back of the book
- Create your own spelling games
- Use each word in a sentence and say them to your teacher

Students may choose their own spelling words this week for their dictionary. They may add their words to the spelling words section in the back of the book.

 **Winning the Race!** Write a sentence describing the winner of the race!

_____
_____
_____

Language Level 3 – Lesson 27

Passover

Mr. Lopez asked the class if they remembered the celebrations, or feasts, that they learned about a few months ago. Claire thought, *"How could we forget Mr. Lopez blowing that big ram's horn for the Feast of Trumpets?!"* He reminded them of the Day of Atonement, where one goat was sacrificed while the other went free. He talked about the Feast of Tabernacles, where God's people camped out for about a week as a reminder that our time here is temporary.

Mr. Lopez explained that there is a very special holiday, or holy day, called Passover. "Most people know this celebration as Easter, but the Bible calls it Passover."

"Do you remember learning about Moses and the Exodus?" Mr Lopez asked. "During the last plague, the angel of death passed over — where we get the word Passover — the homes of those who had killed a lamb and put its blood on their doorway. The first born in those homes did not die."

"God also told the people they were to remove all leaven from their homes and not eat leavened bread for a week." Mr. Lopez explained, "Leaven is yeast and makes bread rise. They had to eat their bread flat. Many believe leaven is a symbol of sin and this reminds us to remove it from our lives."

Mr. Lopez continued, "After that dark Passover night, God's people left Egypt and the bondage of slavery." He then glanced at the clock and realized they were out of time. What a place to end! He encouraged the students to come back next week to hear the best part about Passover. He also said they might want to discuss Passover with their parents and to read, as a family, the Bible's account of the first Passover in Exodus.

Name_____   Exercise 1   Day 136

 **NARRATION PRACTICE**

(1) What celebrations did Mr. Lopez remind the class about?

(2) What special holiday is this story about?

(3) What did God's people do for this holiday?

(4) How does this story end?

 **TEACHER NOTE**
- You may want to read about the Exodus with your students. The full story is covered in chapters 1-13. The tenth plague and the Passover begin at chapter 11. Please use discretion with your children when covering hard topics such as this.

Memorization

Mr. Lopez's class memorized Philippians 4:4–9 and Colossians 3:12–15. See if you can say all the verses at once. It may take some practice!

Grouping

Write a word that goes with the others in each group.

cow : horse : _____

lion : giraffe : _____

maple : pine : _____

bus : car : _____

240   Language Level 3 – Lesson 28

Name_____   Exercise 2   Day 137

 **Review: Proper Nouns, Pronouns**

Do you remember what a proper noun is? A proper noun names a person, place, or thing. A proper noun begins with a capital letter.

Write a sentence using a proper noun.

_____
_____
_____
_____

Did you start your sentence with a capital letter? Did you end it with a punctuation mark? If not, be sure to fix it.

Do you remember what a pronoun is? A pronoun takes the place of a noun.

The pronoun "I" is the type of proper noun that always needs to be capitalized.

Write a sentence using "I" as a pronoun:

_____
_____
_____
_____

Remember: Singular means one. Plural means more than one.

Singular Pronouns	Plural Pronouns
I me you he him she her it	we they them us

Language Level 3 – Lesson 28

Exercise 2 — Day 137

Rewrite the sentences using the correct pronoun for the underlined parts:

(1) <u>Claire</u> loves her cat.

_____

(2) <u>Claire and Ava</u> gave the cat food.

_____

Tell your teacher about some proper nouns in this picture. Also, give a pronoun for each proper noun.

Name _____   Exercise 3   Day 138

Review: Sentences and Punctuation

Do you remember the three different kinds of punctuation marks? They are a period, question mark, and an exclamation point.

Write a sentence that ends with a period.

_____
_____

Write a sentence that ends with a question mark.

_____
_____

Write a sentence that ends with an exclamation point.

_____
_____

Do you remember the four types of sentences? You may need to ask your teacher to help you read their names. They are:

Imperative: a command that ends with a period

Declarative: a statement that ends with a period, too

Exclamatory: an exclamation that has emotion and ends in an exclamation point

Interrogative: a question that ends with a question mark

What kind of sentences are these? Put an **IM** for Imperative, **D** for Declarative, **E** for Exclamatory, and **IN** for Interrogative:

(1) ____ Why did Claire feel sad?

(2) ____ I like going to church.

(3) ____ Stop that car!

(4) ____ Bring me a Bible.

Language Level 3 – Lesson 28

Do you remember how to use commas? Put commas in the right place in each sentence.

Hint: Some sentences have more than one comma.

(5) Bring the dirty clothes here Jin.

(6) Micah saw building blocks a skateboard and games in Jin's room.

(7) Micah please bring the skateboard here.

(8) You God are worthy of praise.

Do you remember what an interjection is? An interjection is a word that expresses emotion or feelings.

Write the correct punctuation mark for the interjection in each sentence.

(9) Wow God is good.

(10) Oh did you finish your math?

Name_____   Exercise 4   Day 139

READING COMPREHENSION

Read pages 64–65 of *101 Favorite Stories from the Bible* with your teacher.

Answer the questions on page 65.

Copy 2 Peter 2:15, then memorize it with your teacher.

Copy the picture on page 65 and color it. Draw the whole picture or only the people. Copy the caption from page 65 below.

Language Level 3 – Lesson 28

Name _____ Exercise 5 Day 140

 **Blends**

We are going to work with words that have the blends ng, nk, nt, pt, sk, and st.

Learn to spell these words:

> crept, feast, hang, kept, prank, skate, stink, strong, test, toast

Write silly sentences until you have used all the spelling words. Put as many words as you can into each sentence.

_____
_____
_____
_____
_____
_____
_____
_____
_____
_____

Circle each of the spelling words in your sentences.

Write your spelling words on notecards. Write one word on each card. You may create right-brain flashcards with your words.

Language Level 3 – Lesson 28

Lesson 29

Title: *Jonah*

Artist: Bill Looney

(1) Who is in this picture?

(2) What is happening in this picture?

(3) What colors are used in this picture?

(4) How does this picture make you feel? Why?

Comprehension

Draw a picture of how you think Jonah felt while he was in the fish:

Draw a picture of how you think Jonah felt after the fish spit him out:

Draw a picture of how you think the fish felt after it spit Jonah out:

Name_____ Exercise 2 Day 142

 **Plural Nouns**

Do you remember what a plural noun is? Yes, more than one person, place, or thing.

Do you remember how to make a plural noun by adding -s and -es to the end of a word?

Remember:

| plural = add s | ends in s, ss, sh, ch, or x = add es |

vowel + y, add s	vowel + o, add s	consonant + o, add es
key = keys	radio = radios	hero = heroes

- There are two exceptions to this rule!

| piano = pianos | photo = photos |

Add -s or -es to the end of the words to make them plural. Study the rules if you aren't sure.

(1) bus_____   (6) photo_____
(2) piano_____   (7) hand_____
(3) church_____   (8) mess_____
(4) box_____   (9) radio_____
(5) bush_____   (10) tomato_____

Language Level 3 – Lesson 29

Exercise 2 — Day 142

If the noun ends in a consonant + y, we change the y to an i and add -es to the end to make it plural.

If the noun ends in an f or fe, we change the f or fe to a v and add -es to the end to make it plural.

There are two exceptions to this rule!

| ⚠ | roof = roofs | cliff = cliffs |

Change these words to make them plural.

(11) city _____   (14) country _____

(12) wolf _____   (15) cliff _____

(13) roof _____   (16) knife _____

Some plural nouns don't follow the rules! They are irregular nouns.

Match the singular nouns with the correct plural noun.

Singular	Plural	Singular	Plural
(17) man	people	(25) deer	fish
(18) woman	men	(26) fish	moose
(19) child	women	(27) sheep	deer
(20) person	children	(28) moose	sheep
(21) goose	oxen	(29) corn	octopi
(22) mouse	cacti	(30) seaweed	corn
(23) ox	geese	(31) octopus	seaweed
(24) cactus	mice		

Language Level 3 – Lesson 29

Name _____   Exercise 3   Day 143

Review: Sentences–Subject, Predicate, Conjunctions, Combining

Do you remember what a subject and a predicate is? The subject is who or what the sentence is about. The predicate is what the subject does or is.

Underline the subject of each sentence. Circle the predicate of each sentence.

(1) The girls ate their lunch.

(2) The cat ran fast.

(3) The corn tasted good.

(4) Dad and I saved the cat.

Do you remember what a conjunction is? Conjunctions are words that join two words or phrases together. Here are some common conjunctions:

> and   but   or   nor   for   so

Use the conjunctions above to complete the sentences. You may use each word more than once!

(5) I love green beans, _____ I am full.

(6) You can either have potatoes _____ squash.

(7) I would like peas _____ carrots.

(8) I want okra, _____ I like asparagus, too.

(9) I do not like sweet potatoes, _____ do I like cucumbers.

(10) I ate my dinner, _____ I could go outside.

Language Level 3 – Lesson 29

Exercise 3 Day 143

Combine the two sentences using a conjunction.

(11) I love to work on math. I love to work on spelling.

_____
_____
_____

JUST 4 FUN!

What's what! Write the name of the pictures in the crossword puzzle. If there is an arrow pointing to the right, it means the word is written from left to right in the squares. If there is an arrow pointing down, that means the word is written down instead of across. The first one is done for you! Have your teacher help you.

252 Language Level 3 – Lesson 29

Name_____ Exercise 4 Day 144

READING COMPREHENSION

Read pages 66–67 of *101 Favorite Stories from the Bible* with your teacher.

Answer the questions on page 67.

Copy Hebrews 10:23, then memorize it with your teacher.

Copy the picture on page 67 and color it. Draw the whole picture or only the people. Copy the caption from page 67 below.

Language Level 3 – Lesson 29

Name_____   Exercise 5   Day 145

 **Blends**

Learn to spell words with the blends ch and tch.

> batch, beach, catch, cheap, chew,
> ditch, itch, peach, reach, scratch

Create your own word search with your spelling words.

- ○ batch
- ○ beach
- ○ catch
- ○ cheap
- ○ chew
- ○ ditch
- ○ itch
- ○ peach
- ○ reach
- ○ scratch

Write your spelling words on notecards. Write one word on each card. You may create right-brain flashcards with your words.

254   Language Level 3 – Lesson 29

 **READING TOGETHER**

Jesus, the Lamb

As the class arrived, they were eager to hear more about Passover. Mr. Lopez jumped right in. "God told the people they were to celebrate the Passover every year. In fact, He said the Passover was to be the start of their year from now on! It must have been a pretty important feast for God to restart their calendar."

Mr. Lopez continued, "Jesus also celebrated the Passover. However, He changed Passover forever. It was during Passover that He gave Himself to be the Passover Lamb. He became the Lamb that died to pay for our sins. He was perfect, without sin, the Holy Son of God. His blood was spilled so that we can be forgiven and set free.

"Isn't God's plan amazing? The Exodus helps us understand the sacrifice Jesus made. We are like the Israelites, stuck in Egypt in the bondage of sin. Jesus was our perfect Lamb. His blood was shed so that we could be forgiven and set free. But we still have to do our part and repent. This is how the leaven, or sin, is removed from our life. When we accept Jesus, we are a new person. In a way, it becomes a new year, and a new life, for us."

As Mr. Lopez dismissed his class, he encouraged them to discuss Passover with their parents and to read, as a family, the Bible's account of how Jesus celebrated and gave His life during Passover in the accounts of Matthew, Mark, Luke, or John.

 **NARRATION PRACTICE**

(1) What surprising thing did God do to the Israelites' calendar?

(2) How did Jesus change Passover forever?

(3) How does Exodus help us to understand the sacrifice of Jesus?

(4) What is our part?

 **TEACHER NOTE**

- You may want to read about the Crucifixion and Resurrection of Jesus with your children. This account is found in Matthew 26-28, Mark 14-16, Luke 22-24, and John 18-20. Please use discretion with your children when covering hard topics such as this.

Name_____ Exercise 1 Day 146

Comprehension

Underline the best topic sentence for this story. Remember, a topic sentence is the first sentence in a paragraph. It tells what the paragraph is about.

All I had to do was flap my arms like a bird to fly a few feet off the ground. When I flapped faster, I would go even higher! I flew above our house, but I got scared and stopped flapping my arms. Before I hit the ground, I woke up.

(1) I love to fly!

(2) Hitting the ground hurts!

(3) I like to take naps.

(4) I had a dream I could fly.

Language Level 3 – Lesson 30

Name_____ Exercise 2 Day 147

Review: Possessive Nouns, Prepositions

Do you remember what a possessive noun is? A possessive noun shows who or what owns or has something.

We make a singular noun possessive by adding an apostrophe and an -s.

When a plural noun ends in an -s, we show ownership by adding only an apostrophe to the end of the word.

Add either ' or 's to each possessive noun:

(1) toys_____

(2) dog_____

(3) cats_____

(4) chick_____

Do you remember the exception to this rule? *Its* is a singular possessive noun, but it does not have an apostrophe and an -s. Only the contraction *it's* has an apostrophe and an -s.

Write *it's* or *its* correctly in the sentences.

(5) The dog lost _____ toy.

(6) _____ under the couch.

Language Level 3 – Lesson 30   257

Exercise 2 — Day 147

Do you remember what a preposition is? A preposition is a word that links a noun (or pronoun) to another word in the sentence. It shows a relationship between a noun and another word.

Prepositions show location. Study these common prepositions:

above	on	inside	in
below	off	outside	to
over	before	with	into
under	after	through	by

Do you remember what a prepositional phrase is? A prepositional phrase begins with a preposition and ends with a noun.

In the sentences below, underline the prepositional phrase then circle the preposition.

(7) The bird flew into the tree.

(8) Claire walked by the garden.

(9) Ava played with Claire's cat.

(10) The ball went over the fence.

Name_____ Exercise 3 Day 148

Review: Quotation Marks

Do you remember what quotation marks are? Quotation marks are used to show exactly what someone said.

Add quotation marks to the sentences below. **Hint:** They go before and after a direct quote.

(1) Mom said, Be nice to each other.

(2) Claire asked, How can we show mercy?

(3) Mr. Lopez said, Jesus was the Passover Lamb.

(4) Ava said, I want my life to start new.

Write a sentence using a quote spoken by someone in your family. Start your sentence with the person's name.

　○ Remember to use a comma before the quote.

　○ Remember to use a capital letter to start the first word of the quote.

　○ Remember to use quotation marks before and after the quote.

_____
_____
_____
_____

Language Level 3 – Lesson 30

Name _____   Exercise 4   Day 149

READING COMPREHENSION

Read pages 68–69 of *101 Favorite Stories from the Bible* with your teacher.

Answer the questions on page 69.

Copy Hebrews 11:30, then memorize it with your teacher.

_____
_____
_____
_____
_____
_____

Copy the picture on page 69 and color it. Draw the whole picture or only the people. Copy the caption from page 69 below.

_____
_____
_____
_____
_____

Name_____   Exercise 5   Day 150

 **Blends**

We are going to work with words that have the blends spr, shr, str, squ, scr, spl, thr.

Read the blends to your teacher:

spr   shr   str   squ   scr   spl   thr

Learn to spell these words:

> scrap, shred, shrink, spray, spread,
> splash, squawk, stray, three, throw

Solve the riddles using the spelling words.

(1) Do this with a ball. _____

(2) A cat or dog without a home. _____

(3) Do this to butter on bread. _____

(4) To make smaller. _____

(5) Loud sound a bird can make. _____

(6) Water can do this when it comes out of a hose. _____

Language Level 3 – Lesson 30

Exercise 5 — Day 150

(7) To tear into a lot of pieces. _____

(8) A small piece of paper. _____

(9) A number. _____

(10) You can do this with water in the pool. _____

Write a fun sentence using at least two of your spelling words. Be sure to start your sentence with a capital letter and end it with a punctuation mark.

_____
_____
_____

Write your spelling words on notecards. Write one word on each card. You may create right-brain flashcards with your words.

Optional Activities

Ask your teacher to read each spelling word. Spell the word out loud to your teacher and use it in a sentence.

Lesson 31

All Things Bright And Beautiful
by Cecil Alexander

All things bright and beautiful,
All creatures great and small,
All things wise and wonderful,
The Lord God made them all.

Each little flower that opens,
Each little bird that sings,
He made their glowing colors,
He made their tiny wings.

The rich man in his castle,
The poor man at his gate,
God made them high and lowly,
And ordered their estate.

The purple headed mountain,
The river running by,
The sunset and the morning,
That brightens up the sky;

The cold wind in the winter,
The pleasant summer sun,
The ripe fruits in the garden,
He made them every one:

The tall trees in the greenwood,
The meadows where we play,
The rushes by the water,
We gather every day;

He gave us eyes to see them,
And lips that we might tell,
How great is God Almighty,
Who has made all things well.

Comprehension
Were there any words you didn't understand? Circle them.

- The teacher should discuss with the student the meaning of the circled words in the context of the poem.

Hymns for Little Children, 1848

Name _____ Exercise 1 Day 151

 **NARRATION PRACTICE**

(1) What is the title of the poem?

(2) When was this poem written?

(3) What is this poem about?

(4) Each section of the poem is called a stanza. There are seven stanzas in this poem. Which stanza is your favorite? Why?

(5) How does this poem make you feel?

Memorization

Memorize at least one stanza of this poem with your teacher.

 **TEACHER NOTE** • Both the teacher and the student should work together to memorize the first stanza of the poem.

Rhyming

Write a rhyming word for each set of sentences.

(6) If I want to touch a star,

I would have to travel _____.

(7) As I dug deep in the ground,

An old toy I have _____.

(8) Out in the woods, I climb a tree.

It is so much fun being _____.

(9) As I look into the creek,

It is a fish that I _____.

Language Level 3 – Lesson 31

Name_____   Exercise 2   Day 152

 **Nouns: Prefix, Root Word, Suffix, Compound Words**

Do you remember what a prefix is? A prefix is letters added to the beginning of a word to change the meaning.

Do you remember what a root word is? The word we add a suffix or a prefix to is called a root word.

Circle the root word, then underline the prefix:

(1) unless

(2) remove

(3) income

(4) distrust

(5) premade

(6) telephone

Do you remember what a suffix is? A suffix is letters added to the end of a word to change the meaning.

We can add the suffix *-ed* and *-ing* to a word.

Remember:

- If the word ends with a silent e, then we drop the e before adding the suffix.
- Where we have a word with one syllable, one short vowel, and ends with one consonant, we must double the consonant then add *-ed* or *-ing*.

Remember these examples:

> jump : jumped, jumping
> race : raced, racing
> silent e = drop the e
>
> pop : popped, popping
> one syllable, one short vowel, ends in one consonant = double the consonant

Language Level 3 – Lesson 31

Exercise 2 — Day 152

Follow the rules you learned to add the suffix *-ed* and *-ing* to each word.

(7) add: _____ _____

(8) taste: _____ _____

(9) rip: _____ _____

We can use the suffix *-er* and *-est* to compare two things.

We add *-er* to a word to show that there is more of something than another.

We add *-est* to a word to show that there is the most of something.

Add the suffix *-er* and *-est* to the following words:

(10) fast: _____ _____

(11) tame: _____ _____

Do you remember what a compound word is? Compound words are made when we take two words and make them into one and create a new meaning.

Match the words to create a compound word:

(12) base   fly

(13) jelly   ball

(14) fire   fish

Name_____ Exercise 3 Day 153

Review: Contractions

Do you remember what a contraction is? Contract means to shrink or shorten. We create a contraction when we take two words, remove some letters, and make them into one word. We use an apostrophe where we took out letters.

Match the contractions to the words:

(1) doesn't   they will   (4) I've   we would
(2) they'll   does not   (5) we'd   must have
(3) how's   how is   (6) must've   I have

Write the correct contractions:

(7) let us _____

(8) do not _____

(9) you are _____

(10) I am _____

Remember, we can abbreviate (shorten) many titles. A title describes a person, their job, or their position. Titles begin with a capital letter. We put a period at the end of an abbreviation.

Match the word with the correct description:

(11) Mister   the title of a married woman
(12) Miss   the title of a man
(13) Missus   the title of an unmarried woman

Language Level 3 – Lesson 31

Exercise 3 — Day 153

Match the titles to the correct abbreviations:

(14) Mister   Ms.
(15) Miss   Mrs.
(16) Missus   Mr.
(17) Doctor   Prof.
(18) Reverend   Dr.
(19) Detective   Rev.
(20) Professor   Det.
(21) Honorable   Sen.
(22) Senator   Pres.
(23) Representative   Hon.
(24) President   Rep.
(25) Captain   Sgt.
(26) General   Capt.
(27) Sergeant   Gen.

Name_____ Exercise 4 Day 154

READING COMPREHENSION

Read pages 70–71 of *101 Favorite Stories from the Bible* with your teacher.

Answer the questions on page 71.

Copy Psalm 50:15, then memorize it with your teacher.

Copy the picture on page 71 and color it. Draw the whole picture or only the people. Copy the caption from page 71 below.

Language Level 3 – Lesson 31

Name_____ Exercise 5 Day 155

 **/f/ Sound Words**

We are going to work with words that make the /f/ sound using -f, -gh, and -ph.

Learn to spell these words:

> cough, fancy, father, fence, form,
> laugh, orphan, phrase, tough, trophy

Use the spelling words to complete the silly sentences. (**Hint**: You can only use each spelling word once.)

(1) The _____ won a _____ for being the most _____ dressed boy at the party.

(2) My _____ put up a _____ to keep the _____ cows in the field.

(3) Don't _____ or _____ while you write a funny _____ on the _____.

Write your spelling words on notecards. Write one word on each card. You may create right-brain flashcards with your words.

Language Level 3 – Lesson 31

 **Lesson 32**

God's Plan

Mr. Lopez started the class by saying they were going to talk more about the feasts that God told His people to celebrate. He said, "The Saturday, or Sabbath, after the Passover was set apart by God. An offering called Firstfruits was to be made that day from the first harvest of food they had grown."

Mr. Lopez then explained, "God told His people that they were to count fifty days from the Firstfruits. On the fiftieth day, they were to make a sacrifice to the Lord.

"After Jesus died on the cross, he was resurrected from the dead. This means he came back to life! Before He went back up to heaven, He spent time with people who knew Him. Luke 33:49 and Acts 1:4 tell us that while He was with the disciples, He told them to wait in Jerusalem until the coming of the Holy Spirit." Mr. Lopez then asked the class, "Can you guess when the Holy Spirit came upon them?" The children weren't sure, so he said, "He came on day fifty! For many, many years, God's people had counted fifty days in anticipation of the Holy Spirit, and they didn't even know it! We call this day Pentecost."

Mr. Lopez closed the class by encouraging them to read about the feasts in Leviticus 23 with their parents. He also said they could read more about the coming of the Holy Spirit in Acts 1-2. As the students filed out of class, Ava said to Claire, "Wow! God always has plan!" Claire agreed and shook her head.

- You may want to read about the feasts with your students in Leviticus 23 and the coming of the Holy Spirit in Acts 1-2.

(1) What is the feast of Firstfruits?
(2) How many days were the people to count?
(3) What does resurrection mean?
(4) What did Jesus tell the disciples to do?
(5) What do we call the day the Holy Spirit came?
(6) Why did Ava say that God always has a plan?

Maps: Street Names and Following Directions!

Look at this map. The streets all have names. Circle the correct answer.

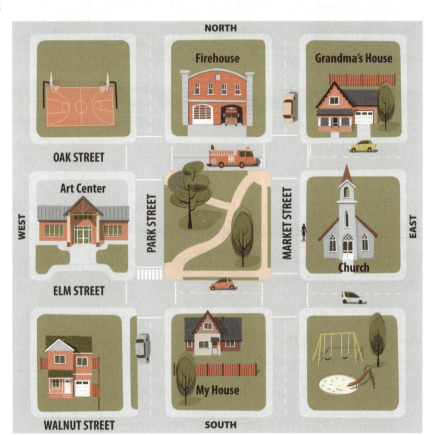

(1) Is the firehouse on Elm Street or Oak Street?

(2) Is the church on Oak Street or Elm Street?

(3) Is my house on Walnut Street or Oak Street?

Write your answer in the blank.

(4) _____ Street goes north from my house to Grandma's House.

(5) _____ Street goes south from the basketball court to the Art Center.

Name_____ Exercise 2 Day 157

 **Review: Verb Usage**

Write a sentence using the verb to show something happened in the past. You will need to change the verb!

runs
_____
_____
_____
_____

jump
_____
_____
_____
_____

Do you remember the 8 state of being verbs? If not, be sure to memorize them. Draw a line from the sentence to the correct state of being verb:

(1) That _____ a fun game.   am

(2) I _____ good at it.   are

(3) We _____ playing the game now.   is

(4) Ava and Claire _____ here yesterday.   was

(5) Micah _____ with Jin.   were

Language Level 3 – Lesson 32   273

Exercise 2 Day 157

(6) Ava and Claire were _____ gentle with the cat.   been

(7) Micah has _____ to Jin's house.   be

(8) The friends will _____ in Sunday school soon.   being

Draw a line from the sentence to the correct verb:

(9) He _____ a cute dog.   have

(10) They _____ fun in the yard.   has

Write a sentence using the verb: had

_____
_____
_____

Draw a line from the sentence to the correct helping verb:

(11) Claire and Ava _____ counted to fifty.   has

(12) Micah _____ helped Jin build a tower.   have

Write a sentence using the helping verb: have

_____
_____
_____

Language Level 3 – Lesson 32

Exercise 2   Day 157

Draw a line from the sentence to the correct verb:

(13) I have _____ Ava study.   see

(14) I _____ her study yesterday.   seen

(15) I _____ Ava study her Bible every Sunday.   saw

Draw a line from the sentence to the correct verb:

(16) I have _____ breakfast already.   eat

(17) I _____ my last orange yesterday.   eaten

(18) I _____ eggs every day.   ate

(19) I will _____ to church tonight.   went

(20) I _____ to church last night.   gone

(21) I have _____ to church every night.   go

Draw a line from the sentence to the correct verb:

(22) Micah and Jin ___ next to each other.   set

(23) Claire _____ the Bible on the desk.   sit

Language Level 3 – Lesson 32

Name _____ Exercise 3 Day 158

Review: Simile

Do you remember what a simile is? A simile compares two different things using the words *like* or *as*.

Here is an example of the two types of similes. The first sentence uses the simile *as*. The second sentence uses the simile *like*:

Micah ate as much as a horse.

Claire sings like an angel.

We call a simile a figure of speech. We say this because Micah didn't really eat as much as a horse. We are saying that he ate a lot.

We can make our sentences fun by using similes.

Finish the sentences using a simile. You may use more than one word:

She is as sweet as _____.

The bee buzzed like _____.

Write a sentence using the simile: as

_____
_____

Write a sentence using the simile: like

_____
_____

Language Level 3 – Lesson 32

Name _____   Exercise 4   Day 159

 **READING COMPREHENSION**

Read pages 72–73 of *101 Favorite Stories from the Bible* with your teacher.

Answer the questions on page 73.

Copy Psalm 118:8, then memorize it with your teacher.

Copy the picture on page 73 and color it. Draw the whole picture or only the people. Copy the caption from page 73 below.

Language Level 3 – Lesson 32

Name _____   Exercise 5   Day 160

 **SPELLING PRACTICE**

-g Words

Learn to spell these words that have the hard and soft g:

> along, edge, engine, game, gentle,
> germ, give, gone, stage, sugar

Word scramble

Unscramble each of the spelling words and write the word spelled correctly.

(1) lgnoa _____   (6) mgea _____

(2) grsua _____   (7) tgsea _____

(3) tlngee _____ (8) gnneei _____

(4) gdee _____   (9) vgei _____

(5) ngoe _____   (10) rmge _____

Write your spelling words on notecards. Write one word on each card. You may create right-brain flashcards with your words.

 CREATE YOUR OWN DICTIONARY!

 **PICTURE STUDY**

Lesson 33

Title: Pastoral Visit (1881)

Artist: Richard Norris Brooke

 **OBSERVATION SKILLS**

(1) What is the name of this painting?

(2) What things do you see in the picture?

(3) What is happening in this painting?

(4) Describe the people in this painting.

(5) What colors are used in this picture?

(6) How does this picture make you feel? Why?

Language Level 3 – Lesson 33

Story Writing

Finish this story about the picture.

It was Saturday night, and everyone was busy cleaning up the house. Mama washed the dishes. Daddy swept the floor. The children dusted and made sure everything was tidy and clean. They had a special guest coming for lunch the next day!

Name _____ Exercise 2 Day 162

 **Review: Word Usage**

Do you remember what an article is? An article comes before a noun. There are three articles: *a, an, the*

Draw a line from the sentence to the correct article:

(1) The pastor came for _____ visit.   an

(2) He gave _____ cat a treat.   the

(3) He ate _____ extra piece of pie.   a

Remember:

	Near	Far
Singular	this	that
Plural	these	those

Draw a line from the sentence to the correct word:

(4) I wore _____ coat.   those

(5) Are _____ my shoes?   that

Write a sentence using: this
_____
_____

Write a sentence using: these
_____
_____

Language Level 3 – Lesson 33   281

Exercise 2 — Day 162

Remember:

| it's = it is | | its = possession (and breaks the rules) |

Draw a line from the sentence to the correct word:

(6) The cat lost _____ toy.   its

(7) I'm sad _____ time to say goodbye.   it's

Remember:

| who's = who is | | whose = possession (and breaks the rules) |

Draw a line from the sentence to the correct word:

(8) _____ jacket is this?   Who's

(9) _____ coming for dinner?   Whose

Name _____   Exercise 3   Day 163

Review: Titles of Books, Movies, and Plays, Dictionary Guide Words

Let's review how to write titles of books, movies, and plays. When you write a sentence using the title of a book, movie, or play, you should:

- Underline the title (or use italics if you are using a computer)
- Capitalize the first and last word
- Capitalize all other words except small words that are not nouns, verbs, or adjectives such as: the, for, and

Underline the titles in the sentences below.

(1) Whale of a Story is a fun book to read.

(2) I was in a play called The Story of Ruth.

(3) Have you watched I Dig Dinosaurs by Buddy Davis?

Write a sentence using the title of a book, movie, or play that you have read or watched.

_____
_____
_____
_____

Language Level 3 – Lesson 33

Dictionary Guide Words

Ask your teacher for a dictionary.

Do you remember what guide words are? They are found at the top of a dictionary page, usually one on each side. They tell you the first and last words that are found on the page. Guide words make it easier to look up words in the dictionary.

TEACHER NOTE
- The student will need a dictionary for this lesson. Also, students may need to review alphabetizing before completing this lesson.

Look at the words with definitions listed on the page of your dictionary. The words on the page are in alphabetical order, between the two guide words.

Open your dictionary to any page. Write the guide words:

_____   _____

Write any two words found on the page in alphabetical order:

_____   _____

Ask your teacher to help you look up these words in your dictionary:
- ○ cave
- ○ river
- ○ swamp

Name_____ Exercise 4 Day 164

READING COMPREHENSION

Read pages 74–75 of *101 Favorite Stories from the Bible* with your teacher.

Answer the questions on page 75.

Copy Psalm 108:13, then memorize it with your teacher.

Copy the picture on page 75 and color it. Draw the whole picture or only the people. Copy the caption from page 75 below.

Language Level 3 – Lesson 33

Name _____ Exercise 5 Day 165

 **Silent Letter Words**

Learn to spell these words that have silent letters:

> castle, gnat, gnaw, knee, knock,
> lamb, thumb, wrestle, wrong, wrote

Find the spelling words in the word search.

- castle
- gnat
- gnaw
- knee
- knock
- lamb
- thumb
- wrestle
- wrong
- wrote

```
W W G B K N E E Z Q T E
D R N N V K P A C H E H
I O A V A T Z C A K T O
L N W S G W R E S T L E
N G D T T N B S T A R G
K N O C K L O G L S W N
T K M S W R O T E T P A
L A M B J M M X W L X T
B I T H U M B U Q E O T
```

Write your spelling words on notecards. Write one word on each card. You may create right-brain flashcards with your words.

 CREATE YOUR OWN DICTIONARY!

286 Language Level 3 – Lesson 33

Lesson 34

Fruit Trees

As the children filed into class, they were excited! Mr. Lopez had surprised them with a special guest. Micah explained to Jin that Mrs. Clark is a missionary to Honduras. He told Jin about the boy their age, Carlos, that Micah wrote letters to. He also told him about how last summer, the church raised money to add onto a playground at the orphanage in Honduras where Carlos lives. Jin couldn't wait to hear more!

Mrs. Clark thanked the children for all their help in raising money for the playground. She then held up pictures of the new equipment. The children were excited to see new slides and swings. Even better were the happy, smiling faces of the children playing.

Micah scanned the pictures for Carlos. Soon, he spotted him holding a toddler as they slid down a slide together. He excitedly pointed Carlos out to Jin as he exclaimed, "Wow! Carlos has grown a lot!" Mrs. Clark laughed at Micah's excitement. She said, "Yes, all of the children have grown a lot. They love to eat!"

"That reminds me," Mrs. Clark continued, "we want to plant fruit trees at the orphanage. Fresh fruit can cost a lot. If we had fruit trees growing at the orphanage, we could give the children fresh fruit more often." Mr. Lopez then told the class that this would be the next fundraiser the church would do for the orphans. He ended the class by saying that next week, Mrs. Clark had a surprise for the class.

(1) What was the surprise Mr. Lopez had for the class?
(2) What did Micah tell Jin about?
(3) Who is Mrs. Clark, and what did she show the class?
(4) What does the church want to do for the orphanage next?

Language Level 3 – Lesson 34

Name _____   Exercise 1   Day 166

Grouping

Write a word that belongs to each group.

(1) cat   hamster   goldfish   _____

(2) tiger   elephant   giraffe   _____

(3) crow   eagle   robin   _____

(4) red   yellow   green   _____

 **Copy!** Copy the picture using the lines to help you. Then below your drawing, give your hamster a name!

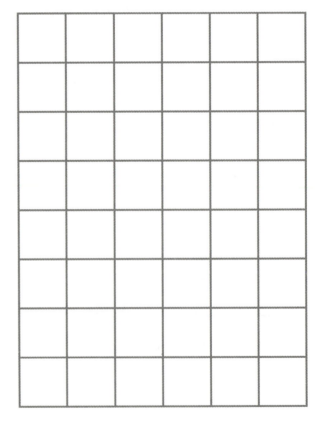

Language Level 3 – Lesson 34

Name_____ Exercise 2 Day 167

Review: Adjectives, Adverbs

Do you remember what an adjective is? An adjective is a word that describes a noun.

We learned that:
- An adjective can describe the *color*, *size*, or *shape* of a noun.
- An adjective can describe how a noun *tastes*, *smells*, or *sounds*.
- An adjective can describe how a noun *looks* or *feels* or *how many*.
- An adjective can describe the *weather*, *feelings*, or *behavior* of a noun.

Here is an example:

Micah got a new, red shirt for his birthday.

Write a sentence using at least two adjectives:
_____
_____
_____
_____

Write a sentence using at least two new adjectives:
_____
_____
_____
_____

Language Level 3 – Lesson 34

Exercise 2 Day 167

Adverbs

Do you remember what an adverb is? Adverbs are similar to adjectives, but instead of describing a noun, they tell about a verb. An adverb often ends in -ly and describes *how*, *when*, *where*, or *how often* a verb happens.

There are many adverbs. Do you remember this list of adverbs?

How	When	Where	How Often
gently	early	above	daily
quickly	now	inside	never
quietly	soon	here	often
sadly	tomorrow	outside	usually
safely	yesterday	upstairs	yearly

Pick an adverb from one of the columns. Write a sentence using that adverb.

_____
_____
_____
_____

Pick an adverb from a different column. Write a sentence using that adverb.

_____
_____
_____
_____

Language Level 3 – Lesson 34

Review: Writing a Paragraph

Do you remember how writing a paragraph is like making a sandwich?

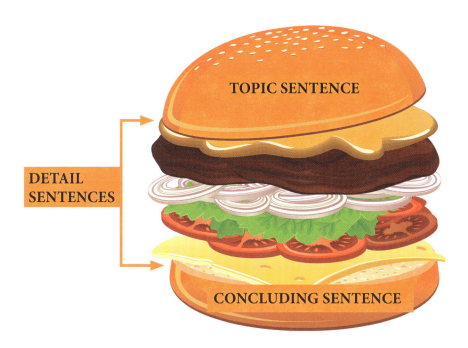

Pretend you are Micah writing a letter to Carlos. What would you say? Would you tell him about your family? Would you ask him about life in Honduras? Write a paragraph to Carlos.

Check off each part as you write your paragraph:

- ○ Write the topic sentence. Remember to indent your topic sentence.
- ○ Write 2-3 sentences that give details about your topic.
- ○ Write a concluding sentence.

Exercise 3 — Day 168

Dear Carlos,

_____

Did you use a capital letter to start each sentence? Did you use correct punctuation at the end of each sentence? Good job!

Name_____   Exercise 4   Day 169

 **READING COMPREHENSION**

Read pages 76–77 of *101 Favorite Stories from the Bible* with your teacher.

Answer the questions on page 77.

Copy Joshua 24:15b, then memorize it with your teacher.

Copy the picture on page 77 and color it. Draw the whole picture or only the people. Copy the caption from page 77 below.

Language Level 3 – Lesson 34

Name_____   Exercise 5   Day 170

 **Double Consonant Words**

We are going to work with words that have double consonants.

Learn to spell these words:

> class, current, dress, fiddle, follow, full, little, matter, tall, wiggle

Write the spelling words in the correct boxes. **Note:** Some words have the same shape.

(1) 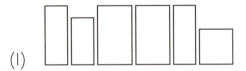   (6)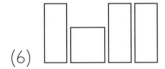

(2)    (7)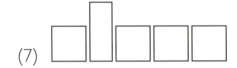

(3)    (8)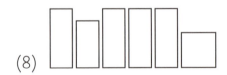

(4) 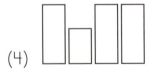   (9)

(5) 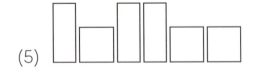   (10)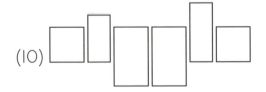

Write your spelling words on notecards. Write one word on each card. You may create right-brain flashcards with your words.

 CREATE YOUR OWN DICTIONARY!

Language Level 3 – Lesson 34

 **READING TOGETHER**

Psalm 67

God be gracious to us and bless us,

And cause His face to shine upon us — Selah.

²That Your way may be known on the earth,

Your salvation among all nations.

³Let the peoples praise You, O God;

Let all the peoples praise You.

⁴Let the nations be glad and sing for joy;

For You will judge the peoples with uprightness

And guide the nations on the earth. Selah.

⁵Let the peoples praise You, O God;

Let all the peoples praise You.

⁶The earth has yielded its produce;

God, our God, blesses us.

⁷God blesses us,

That all the ends of the earth may fear Him.

Comprehension

Were there any words you didn't understand? Circle them.

 **TEACHER NOTE**
- The teacher should discuss with the student the meaning of the circled words in the context of the psalm.

 **NARRATION PRACTICE**

(1) What chapter of Psalms did you read?

(2) How many verses are there in this chapter?

(3) What is this psalm about?

(4) What did you learn about God in this psalm?

(5) What were your favorite verses? Why?

Name _____   Exercise **1**   Day 171

Memorization

Memorize with your teacher at least four verses of this poem. The verses should be in a row and may be picked by you or your teacher.

Rhyming

Write a rhyming word for each set of sentences.

(1) The little bird gave a tweet, _____
  And I thought that it sounded _____.

(2) I love to slowly walk that way. _____
  I wish I could be gone all _____.

(3) I love to drive along the coast. _____
  It is where I visit _____.

(4) When I drink a glass of milk, _____
  It goes down as smooth as _____.

296   Language Level 3 – Lesson 35

Name_____   Exercise 2   Day 172

 **Review: Homonyms, Homophones, Synonyms, Antonyms**

Do you remember what homophones are? Homophones are two words that sound the same. Homophones have different meanings. They are not spelled the same. Remember:

> Homophones
> · sound the same
> · different meanings
> · spelled differently

The words *to*, *too*, and *two* all sound the same, but they have different meanings. Match the homophones with the correct meaning.

(1) to   number
(2) too   also or a lot
(3) two   direction

The words *there*, *their*, and *they're* all sound the same, but they have different meanings.

Match the homophones with the correct meaning.

(4) there   belonging to others
(5) their   they are
(6) they're   a place

Language Level 3 – Lesson 35   297

Exercise 2 — Day 172

Homonyms are two words that sound the same.

Homonyms have different meanings.

They are spelled the same.

Remember:

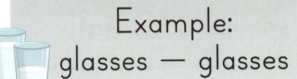

Homonyms
- sound the same
- different meanings
- spelled the same

Example:
glasses — glasses

Choose from the homonyms to write two sentences. Remember to use a different meaning for each homonym. You may ask your teacher for help if you aren't sure of the two meanings.

block : block   wave : wave   scale : scale

_____
_____
_____
_____

Exercise 2   Day 172

Match homophones and homonyms to each correct description. (**Hint:** Each word has more than one answer.)

(7) homophones
(8) homonyms

sound the same
different meaning
same spelling
different spelling

Do you remember what synonyms and antonyms are?

Synonyms are two words that mean the same thing.

Antonyms are two words that have opposite meanings.

Match the synonyms!

(9) sour — glad
(10) happy — tart
(11) leave — come
(12) jump — go
(13) arrive — hop

Match the antonyms!

(14) leave — glad
(15) sad — slow
(16) wet — arrive
(17) fast — cry
(18) laugh — dry

Language Level 3 – Lesson 35

Name_____ Exercise **3** Day 173

4th Quarter Review
(Each question is 4 points)

TEACHER NOTE • Give student access to the Study Sheets in the back of the book while completing this Review.

What kind of sentences are these?

Put an **IM** for Imperative, **D** for Declarative, **E** for Exclamatory and **IN** for Interrogative:

(1) ____ Why should we praise God?

(2) ____ I like to sing at church.

(3) ____ God is good!

(4) ____ Open your Bible to Genesis.

Put commas in the right place in each sentence. (**Hint:** some sentences have more than one comma.)

(5) I will praise you God.

(6) We had salad chicken and fruit at the church picnic.

(7) Micah please read Psalm 67 to the class.

(8) You God are worthy of praise.

Write the correct punctuation mark for the interjection in each sentence.

(9) Wow God is good.

(10) Oh did you finish reading Psalm 67?

Language Level 3 – Lesson 35

Exercise 3 — Day 173

Underline the subject of the sentence. Circle the predicate of the sentence.

(11) The girls ate their lunch.

(12) Write a sentence using a conjunction: and but or nor for so

_____
_____
_____
_____

Add quotation marks to the sentences below.

(13) Mom said, Be nice to each other.

Write the correct contractions:

(14) does not _____

(15) we are _____

(16) I have _____

Match the titles to the correct abbreviations:

(17) Mister   Ms.   (20) Doctor   Det.
(18) Miss   Mrs.   (21) Reverend   Dr.
(19) Missus   Mr.   (22) Detective   Rev.

Language Level 3 – Lesson 35

Exercise 3 — **Day 173**

(23) Write a sentence using the simile: as

_____

- -

(24) Write a sentence using the simile: like

_____

- -

(25) Write a sentence using the title of a book, movie, or play that you have read or watched.

_____

- -

_____

- -

_____

- -

Name _____ Exercise 4 Day 174

 **READING COMPREHENSION**

Read pages 78–79 of *101 Favorite Stories from the Bible* with your teacher.

Answer the questions on page 79.

Copy Psalm 101:6a, then memorize it with your teacher.

Copy the picture on page 79 and color it. Draw the whole picture or only the people. Copy the caption from page 79 below.

Language Level 3 – Lesson 35

Name _____ Exercise 5 Day 175

 **Ordinal Number Words, 1-10**

Learn to spell these ordinal number words. Ordinal numbers show place. If you are the second person in line, you are in the second place.

 The teacher may want to spend some time talking about ordinal numbers.

> first, second, third, fourth, fifth, sixth, seventh, eighth, ninth, tenth

Create your own word search with your spelling words.

- first
- second
- third
- fourth
- fifth
- sixth
- seventh
- eighth
- ninth
- tenth

Write your spelling words on notecards. Write one word on each card. You may create right-brain flashcards with your words.

Language Level 3 – Lesson 35

Thank You!

As each student came into class, Mr. Lopez and Mrs. Clark greeted them with an envelope with their name on it.

Micah quickly tore open his letter and read:

> May 1, 2021
>
> Dear Micah,
>
> Thank you so much for working so hard to raise money for our playground. All of us are so happy to have new slides and swings. Now, all of the children can play on the playground at the same time.
>
> Did you see the picture of me and my little brother on the slide? His name is Diego. We went down the slide that day at least a hundred times. He never got tired of it.
>
> I hope one day I can thank you in person.
>
> Your Friend,
> Carlos

Micah was so happy to hear from Carlos. He was excited about the new playground, too. As he looked up from his letter, he noticed Jin reading a letter. Micah was surprised since Jin was new and didn't have a pen pal in Honduras yet. Jin explained that Mrs. Clark said there were extra letters. Jin then showed Micah a sweet picture of what looked like a child going down a slide. There was a note on the other side from Carlos. It said that Diego had drawn the picture as a thank you.

As the boys left class together, Jin told Micah that he was going to draw Diego a picture of one of his LEGO™ creations. They were excited they shared brothers for penpals.

 **NARRATION PRACTICE**

(1) What did Mrs. Clark have for the students?

(2) What did Micah's letter say?

(3) What did Jin have that surprised Micah?

(4) Why were Micah and Jin excited?

OBSERVATION SKILLS

Study the picture, then write a paragraph telling a story about the picture. Be sure to use ideas from the picture for your story.

You may want to think about these questions before you start to write:

- Where does the picture take place?
- Who is in the picture?
- What are they doing?
- What else do you see in the picture?
- What is at the top of the picture? How about the middle? How about the bottom?

Exercise 1　Day 176

Check off each part as you write your paragraph:
- ○ Write the topic sentence. Remember to indent your topic sentence.
- ○ Write 2-3 sentences that give details about your topic.
- ○ Write a concluding sentence.

Name_____   Exercise 2   Day 177

4th Quarter Review
(Each question is 4 points)

TEACHER NOTE • Give student access to the Study Sheets in the back of the book while completing this Review.

(1) Rewrite the sentence using the correct pronoun for the underlined parts:

<u>Claire and Ava</u> gave the cat food.
_____
_____

Add -s or -es to the end of the words to make them plural.

(2) photo_____   (4) tomato_____

(3) mess_____

Change these words to make them plural.

(5) city _____   (7) roof _____

(6) wolf _____

Add either ' or 's to each possessive noun.

(8) dog_____   (9) cats_____

Write it's or its correctly in the sentences.

(10) The dog lost _____ toy.

(11) _____ under the couch.

308   Language Level 3 – Lesson 36

Exercise 2 — Day 177

In the sentences below, underline the prepositional phrase, then circle the preposition.

(12) Ava played with Claire's cat.

Circle the root word, then underline the prefix:

(13) income

Add the suffix *-er* and *-est* to the following words:

(14) fast: _____ _____

(15) tame: _____ _____

Draw a line from the sentence to the correct verb:

(16) Ava likes to _____ next to Claire.   set

(17) Claire _____ the Bible on the desk.   sit

Draw a line from the sentence to the correct word:

(18) I wore _____ coat.   those

(19) Are _____ my shoes?   that

Draw a line from the sentence to the correct word:

(20) _____ jacket is this?   Who's

(21) _____ coming for dinner? Whose

Language Level 3 – Lesson 36

Exercise 2   Day 177

(22) Write a sentence using an adjective.

_____
_____
_____
_____

(23) Write a sentence using an adverb.

_____
_____
_____
_____

Match homophones and homonyms to each correct description. (**Hint:** Each word has more than one answer.)

(24) homophones
(25) homonyms

sound the same
different meaning
same spelling
different spelling

Writing a Letter

Study the letter Carlos wrote to Micah. The main part of his letter is called the body.

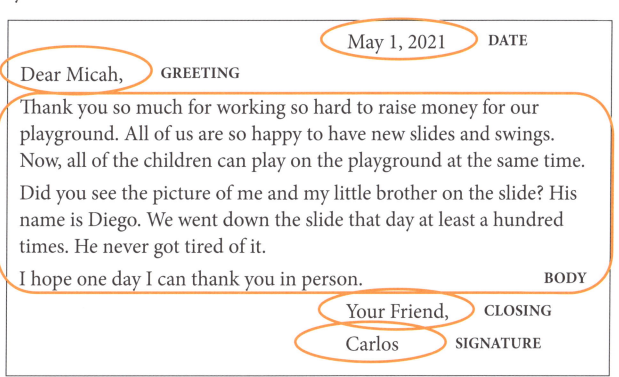

Have you had a friend or family member do something nice for you or give you a gift? Write a thank you letter to a friend or family member. Ask your teacher for paper and an envelope for your letter.

Be sure to put the parts of your letter in the correct place:

- date
- greeting
- body
- closing
- signature

When you write the body of your letter, remember to use what you learned about writing paragraphs.

Exercise 3 — Day 178

Check off each part as you write your paragraph:
- ○ Write the topic sentence. Remember to indent your topic sentence.
- ○ Write 2-3 sentences that give details about your topic.
- ○ Write a concluding sentence.

Be sure to:
- ○ Correctly capitalize your words
- ○ Use correct punctuation

Addressing the Envelope

Now, it is time to put the address on your envelope and mail it! Follow the example for writing addresses on an envelope. Ask your teacher for help.

Language Level 3 – Lesson 36

Name_____ Exercise 4   Day 179

 READING COMPREHENSION

Read pages 80–81 of *101 Favorite Stories from the Bible* with your teacher.

Answer the questions on page 81.

Copy Psalm 1:6, then memorize it with your teacher.

_____
_____
_____
_____
_____
_____

Copy the picture on page 81 and color it. Draw the whole picture or only the people. Copy the caption from page 81 below.

_____
_____
_____
_____
_____
_____

Name_____ Exercise 5 Day 180

 **Spelling Review**

Use your flashcards to practice your spelling words.

You may:

- Ask someone to quiz you on how to spell the words
- Play spelling games found in the back of the book
- Create your own spelling games
- Use each word in a sentence and say them to your teacher

Students may choose their own spelling words this week for their dictionary. They made add their words to the spelling words section in the back of the book.

Congratulations! You have finished the course.

Teacher Aids

How to use this section

These pages are included for the teacher to provide to the student. The teacher may make copies of the practice pages, or they can be laminated (or put in page protectors) and used with dry erase markers.

Study sheets are for the student to use for reference and for further study as needed.

The activities and games are fun ideas to use with lessons or for extra practice.

Table of Contents:

For the Teacher

Assessment Charts	319
Independent Reading List	323
Recommended Book List for Reading Practice	325
Create Your Own Dictionary!	327
Activities and Games	331
Spelling Practice	345

For the Student

Spelling List	347
Spelling Words	349
Sight Words	355
Copywork Practice	359
Days of the Week Practice	368
Months of the Year Practice	369
Ordinal Number Practice	371
Contraction Practice	372
Titles Practice	373
Calendar Study Sheets	374
Grammar Study Sheets	376

Answer Key

Worksheet Answers	393

Assessments

Assessments

We have provided Quarterly Reviews within the curriculum at the end of each quarter. Each quarter has two Reviews covering punctuation, grammar, and writing. There is also a spelling Review. The three Reviews provided each quarter may be used as quizzes or tests for grading purposes.

Grading Options for This Course:

It is always the option of an educator to assess student grades however he or she might deem best. For Language Lessons, the teacher may evaluate whether a student has mastered a particular skill or whether the student needs additional experience. A teacher may rank these on a five-point scale as follows:

Skill Mastered Needs Experience

5 (equals an A) 4 (B) 3 (C) 2 (D) 1 (equals an F)

A — Student shows complete mastery of concepts with no errors.

B — Student shows mastery of concepts with minimal errors.

C — Student shows partial mastery of concepts. Review of some concepts is needed.

D — Student shows minimal understanding of concepts. Review is needed.

F — Student does not show understanding of concepts. Review is needed.

First Semester Assessment Chart

		Skill Mastered	Needs Experience
	First Quarter		
Week 1	Grouping, Alphabet, Vowels		
	Alphabet, Vowels, Consonants		
	Sentences: Capitalization, Punctuation, Types		
	Short -a, -e Words (ask, basket, candy, damp, stand, check, every, help, left, next); Dictionary		
Week 2	Sight Words: Review		
	Proper Nouns: People, Places, Things		
	Calendar		
	Short -i, -o, -u Words (admit, drink, slip, adopt, doctor, pond, lunch, such, under, until); Dictionary		
Week 3	Sight Words Practice		
	Proper Nouns (I), Pronouns (I, you, he, him, she, her, it, me, we, they, them, we, us)		
	Calendar: Days of the Week, Abbreviations		
	Long -a Pattern Words (away, pray, today, brain, nail, raise, sail, game, state, take); Dictionary		
Week 4	Memorizing, Sight Words		
	Plural Nouns: -s, -es		
	Calendar: Months, Abbreviations		
	Long -e Pattern Words (clean, meal, seat, keep, need, sleep, breeze, theme, baby, easy); Dictionary		
Week 5	Grouping, Memorizing, Related Words, Sight Words		
	Plural Nouns: + y, Vowel + o, Consonant + o, Exceptions		
	Types of Sentences, Interjections		
	Long -i Pattern Words (child, quiet, pilot, sign, light, sigh, bike, dime, hydrant, July); Dictionary		
Week 6	Story Writing		
	Plural Nouns: Consonant + y, f or fe, Exceptions		
	Commas: in a List, Personal Address		
	Long -o Pattern Words (cold, most, open, road, moan, alone, woke, hope, grow, yellow); Dictionary		
Week 7	Syllables		
	Nouns: Plural, Irregular		
	People: Initials and Title Abbreviations		
	Long -u Pattern Words (music, truth, grew, newt, noon, root, took, huge, tune, juice); Dictionary		
Week 8	Memorizing, Picture Observation		
	Possessive, Plural Possessive Nouns		
	Sentences: Compound Subject, Subject/Predicate		
	Sight Words (about, done, eight, laugh, much, myself, seven, shall, start, today); Dictionary		
Week 9	Rhyming		
	1st Quarter Review		
	1st Quarter Review		
	1st Quarter Spelling Review		

Language Level 3 – Assessments

		Skill Mastered	Needs Experience
	Second Quarter		
Week 1	Maps/Directions		
	Action Verbs		
	Combining Sentences, Conjunctions		
	-ed, -ing Words (pushed, dragged, stopped, saved, cried, boasting, hoping, hopping, using, trying); Dictionary		
Week 2	Comprehension		
	State of Being Verbs (is, am, are, was, were, be, been, being)		
	Compound Words		
	-oy and -oi Words (avoid, coil, choice, moist, poison, destroy, enjoy, royal, oyster, voyage); Dictionary		
Week 3	Memorizing, Word Challenge		
	Adjectives (color, size, shape, taste, smells, sounds, looks, feels, how many, weather, feeling, behavior)		
	Contractions		
	-ar, -or, -er, -ir, -ur Words (lunar, first, dirty, shirt, never, offer, world, mayor, hurt, rural); Dictionary		
Week 4	Memorizing, Rhyming		
	Adverbs		
	Sentences: Quotation Marks		
	Plural -s, -es Words (begins, books, knees, keys, horses, tables, boxes, catches, inches, pinches); Dictionary		
Week 5	Story Writing		
	Prepositions		
	Titles: Books, Magazines, Movies, Plays		
	Plural f to v, y to i Words (leaves, loaves, knives, shelves, thieves, babies, copies, families, flies, ladies, nineties); Dictionary		
Week 6	Story Writing		
	Homophones (to, too, two)		
	Dictionary Guide Words		
	Irregular Plural Words (cacti, children, corn, deer, fish, geese, mice, people, sheep, woman); Dictionary		
Week 7	Word Categories, Short Story		
	Homophones (there, their, they're)		
	Sentences Review		
	Compound Words (airplane, anything, bookcase, breakfast, everyone, hallway, inside, keyboard, rainbow, sunshine); Dictionary		
Week 8	Matching, Memorizing		
	Articles (a, an, the)		
	Sentences: Writing a Paragraph		
	Contractions (can't, I'm, he's, it'll, let's, she'd, they're, we've, won't, you're); Dictionary		
Week 9	Fact vs. Opinion		
	2nd Quarter Review		
	2nd Quarter Review		
	2nd Quarter Spelling Review		

Language Level 3 – Assessments

Second Semester Assessment Chart

		Skill Mastered	Needs Experience
	Third Quarter		
Week 1	Memorize Philippians 4:4–5, Write a Story		
	Verbs (has, have, had)		
	Combining Sentences		
	-air, -are, -oar, -ore, -ure Words (dairy, hair, care, mare, board, soar, before, shore, cure, future); Dictionary		
Week 2	Rhyming		
	Helping Verbs (has, have, had)		
	Synonyms, Antonyms, Thesaurus		
	pl, pr, sh, th Words (play, plow, press, prison, shut, shape, shingle, that, then, thank); Dictionary		
Week 3	Memorize Philippians 4:6–7, Maps/directions		
	Word Usage Verbs (see, saw, seen)		
	Homonyms, Homophones		
	ck, ct, ft, ld, mp, nd Words (brick, check, inspect, loft, swift, mold, camp, pump, mend, pond); Dictionary		
Week 4	Memorizing, Rhyming		
	Word Usage Verbs (eat, ate, eaten, go, went, gone)		
	Prefix un-, re-		
	Homophones (meat, meet, knows, nose, pair, pear, peace, piece, stair, stare); Dictionary		
Week 5	Story Writing		
	Word Usage (most, almost, sit, set)		
	Prefix in-, im-, dis-, pre-, tele-		
	Homonyms (can, duck, fly, leaves, light, match, pitcher, ring, ruler, yard); Dictionary		
Week 6	Story Writing		
	Word Usage (this, that, these, those)		
	Suffix -ed, -ing, Root Words		
	Prefix dis-, im-, in-, re-, un- Words (discover, dislike, impolite, immature, intake, inactive, reheat, return, undone, unpack); Dictionary		
Week 7	Memorize Colossians 3:12–13, Fact or Fiction		
	Word Usage (it's, its, who's, whose)		
	Simile		
	Suffix -est, -ied, -less, -ly, -y Words (biggest, closest, copied, carried, endless, useless, directly, finally, healthy, thirsty); Dictionary		
Week 8	Memorizing, Write a Psalm		
	Comparison -er, -est		
	Sentences: Writing a Paragraph		
	Roots bio, graph, phon, scope Words (biology, biopsy, biography, autograph, graph, photograph, phone, symphony, scope, microscope); Dictionary		
Week 9	Classifying Words		
	3rd Quarter Review		
	3rd Quarter Review		
	3rd Quarter Spelling Review		

Language Level 3 – Assessments

	Fourth Quarter	Skill Mastered	Needs Experience
Week 1	Memorization, Grouping		
	Review: Nouns (proper, pronouns)		
	Review: Sentences (types, punctuation: commas, interjections)		
	ng, nk, nt, pt, sk, st Words (crept, feast, hang, kept, prank, skate, stink, strong, test, toast); Dictionary		
Week 2	Comprehension		
	Review: Nouns (plural, irregular plural)		
	Review: Sentences (subject/predicate, compound subject, combining, conjunctions)		
	ch, -tch Words (beach, cheap, chew, peach, reach, batch, catch, ditch, itch, scratch); Dictionary		
Week 3	Comprehension		
	Review: Prepositions		
	Sentences: Quotation Marks		
	spr, shr, str, squ, scr, spl, thr Words (spray, spread, shred, shrink, stray, squawk, scrap, splash, three, throw); Dictionary		
Week 4	Memorization, Rhyming		
	Review: Prefix, Suffix, Root Words, Compound Words		
	Review: Contractions, Titles, Abbreviations		
	f, gh, ph Words (form, fancy, father, fence, laugh, trophy, orphan, phrase, tough, cough); Dictionary		
Week 5	Maps/directions		
	Review: Verbs (action, state of being, helping)		
	Review: Similes		
	Soft and Hard g Words (gentle, germ, edge, engine, stage, along, game, give, gone, sugar); Dictionary		
Week 6	Story Writing		
	Review: Word Usage		
	Review: Titles, Dictionary Guide Words		
	Silent Letter Words (castle, lamb, thumb, knee, knock, gnaw, gnat, wrestle, wrong, wrote; dictionary		
Week 7	Grouping		
	Review: Adjectives, Adverbs		
	Review: Writing a Paragraph		
	Double Consonant Words (class, current, dress, fiddle, follow, full, little, matter, tall, wiggle); Dictionary		
Week 8	Memorization, Rhyming		
	Review: Synonyms, Antonyms, Homonyms, Homophones		
	4th Quarter Review		
	Ordinal Number Words (first, second, third, fourth, fifth, sixth, seventh, eighth, ninth, tenth); Dictionary		
Week 9	Observation, Story Writing		
	4th Quarter Review		
	Thank You Letter (date, greeting, body, closing, envelope)		
	4th Quarter Spelling Review		

Independent Reading List

Be sure to keep a record of the books your student is reading. There are spaces below for title, author, and the date of completion. It can be a positive experience as they see this list being filled in and know that they are mastering the important skill of reading. It can be helpful to know the authors and/or specific topics your student expresses interest in by allowing them to help make choices in selecting books. These selections should be fun for the student!

Book Title	Author	Date Completed

Language Level 3 – Independent Reading List

Book Title	Author	Date Completed

Recommended Book List for Reading Practice

All books listed are published by Master Books or New Leaf Publishing Group.

Please select books that match your student's reading level. The books in each group are listed alphabetical, not according to the reading level.

Early Learner Board Books

A is for Adam
All God's Children
D is for Dinosaur
Inside Noah's Ark 4 Kids
It's Designed to Do What It Does Do
My Creation Bible
My Take-Along Bible
N is for Noah
Remarkable Rescue
Silver Ship-Great Creatures
When You See a Rainbow

Early Learner Books Grades K-3

44 Animals of the Bible
Big Thoughts for Little Thinkers–Gospel
Big Thoughts for Little Thinkers–Missions
Big Thoughts for Little Thinkers–Scripture
Big Thoughts for Little Thinkers–Trinity
Charlie & Trike
Cool Creatures of the Ice Age
The Creation Story for Children
Dinosaurs: Stars of the Show
God is Really, Really Real
The Not So Super Skyscraper
Not too Small at All
A Special Door
Tower of Babel
The True Account of Adam & Eve
The True Story of Noah's Ark
Whale of a Story
What Really Happened to the Dinosaurs?
When Dragon Hearts were Good

Grades 4-6 Books

Answers Book for Kids, Vol. 1–8
The Complete Creation Museum Adventure
Dinosaurs by Design
Dinosaurs for Kids
Dinosaurs of Eden
Dry Bones and Other Fossils
God's Amazing Creatures and Me
How Many Animals Were on the Ark?
Inside Noah's Ark–Why it Worked
Life in the Great Ice Age
Marvels of Creation–Birds
Marvels of Creation–Mammals
Marvels of Creation–Sea Creatures
Men of Science, Men of God
Noah's Ark and the Ararat Adventure
Noah's Ark: Thinking Outside the Box
Operation Rawhide
The Story of In God We Trust
The Story of The Pledge of Allegiance
What's so Hot about the Sun?
Why is Keiko Sick?

Recommended Book List for Reading Practice (cont.)

Grades 7-8 Books

The 10-Minute Bible Study
The Building of the ARK Encounter
Champions of Invention
Champions of Mathematics
Champions of Science
Dragons of the Deep
Footprints in the Ash
The Great Alaskan Dinosaur Adventure
Great for God
I Am Ruth
If Animals Could Talk
Life Before Birth
Quick Answers to Tough Questions
Uncovering the Mysteries of the Woolly Mammoth

Create Your Own Dictionary!

The teacher may print off enough copies of the dictionary pages for each student to use for the course. A copy of all the dictionary pages may also be found on our website: www.masterbooks.com/classroom-aids.

The student may write the word, draw a picture, and write a simple definition for each entry.

Language Level 3 – Create Your Own Dictionary!

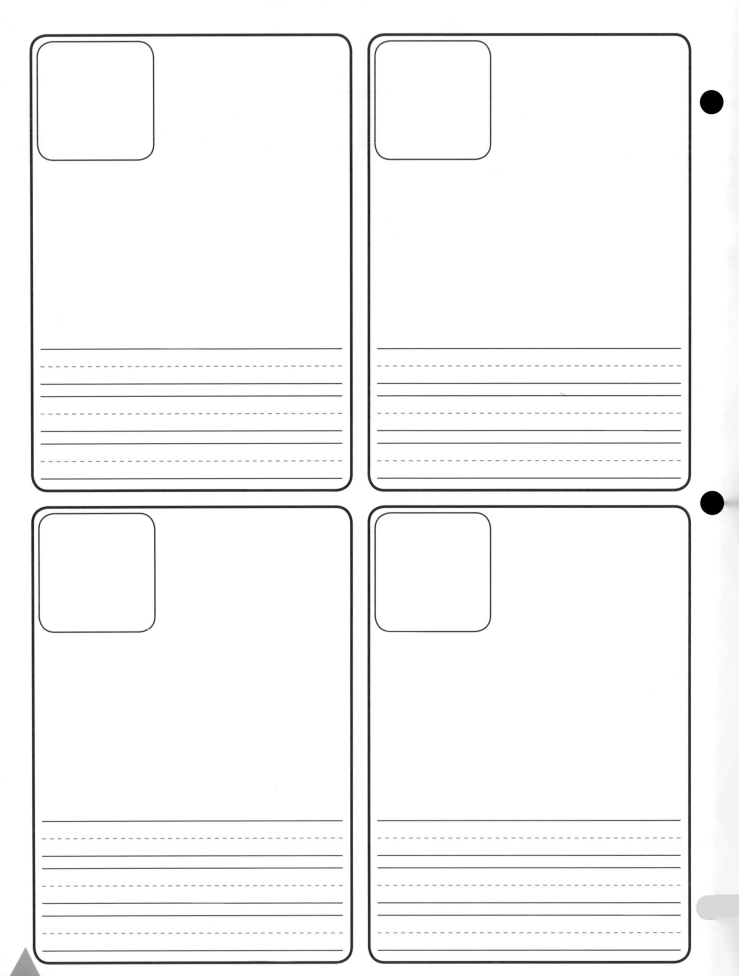

Language Level 3 – Create Your Own Dictionary!

Activities and Games

These games and activities are meant to add extra practice and fun to the lessons. They are optional, but most students will want to do as many as they can.

We encourage the student to create the cards used in the games. Writing out the words on the cards is part of the learning process.

The activities and games are in the order they are introduced in the course. Some games may have variations that cover concepts learned later in the course.

Supplies:
- Index cards
- Markers, crayons, stickers, etc.
- Three-hole punch and rings, or clips to store index cards (optional)

I Spy Game

Focus:
- Nouns, Adjectives, Observation

Number of Players:
- Two or more

Game Play:
- The "spy" says, "I spy with my little eyes something . . ." then goes on to describe an object (noun) that is in the room.
- The other players try to guess what noun the person has spied by asking questions such as "Is it red?" or "Is it something you wear?"
- The game ends when the noun is discovered.

Game Variations:
- The spy must use adjectives to describe the object.
- Give each player a sheet of paper. Have the student create three columns by writing "person," "place," and "thing" across the top of the page. Each time a noun is discovered, have the students write the word under the correct column.
- Have the student write down the adjectives used. When the game is over, have them group the adjectives according to type, color, size, etc.
- Play the game normally, except have the spy use prepositions to describe the object. Example: "I spy with my little eyes something *over* the door."

Days of the Week (Months of the Year) Memory Matching Game

Focus:
- Days of the Week, Months of the Year, Memory, Syllables

Number of Players:
- One or more

Game Play:
- Have students write the days of the week on index cards — one day per card.
- Ask students what they do on Sunday. Have them draw it on a card. Continue with the remaining days until they have 14 cards — seven with the names of the week and seven with what they do each day.
- Turn the cards over and arrange them and play the memory game, matching the days with the student's drawings.
- When the game is over, have the student arrange the days of the week in order.

Bonus Challenge:
- Each time the student turns over a Day of the Week card, have them clap the syllables as they read it.

Game Variation:
- Repeat using the Months of the Year. Have students draw weather-related pictures for each month, including things they do.
- Have students write the names of the days of the week and/or months of the year on one set of notecards and their abbreviations on a second set. Mix them up and play the matching game.

Jumping Bean Days of the Week (Months of the Year, etc.)

Focus:

- Days of the Week, Months of the Year, Memory, Physical Activity

Number of Players:

- One or more

Game Play:

- Gather the seven Days of the Week cards. Mix them up and spread them on the floor, face up. Cards should not touch. They may be taped to the floor using painter's tape.
- Have the student jump from card to card in the correct order, starting with Sunday.

Bonus Challenge:

- Each time the student lands on a day, they should shout out the name of the day.

Game Variations:

- Use the Months of the Year cards and repeat the game. As a bonus challenge, have the student shout out the number of days in that month when they land on it.

Simon Says Nouns, Proper Nouns, Pronouns

Focus:

- Nouns, Proper Nouns, Pronouns, Auditory Perception, Physical Activity

Number of Players:

- Two or more

Game Play:

- Each student should stand in front of a chair. "Simon" stands facing the student(s). Simon says a noun. If it is a proper noun, the student stays standing. If it is a common noun, the student sits. If the student sits when they should stand (or vice-versa), they are out. The last student standing wins. Pick a new Simon and play again!

Game Variations:

- When there are only two players, track how many nouns the player gets right in a row. Work to beat the highest record.
- Play the game using proper nouns and pronouns. The student should stand for the proper nouns and sit for the pronouns.

Action Verb Charades

Focus:
- Action Verbs, Physical Activity

Number of Players:
- Two or more

Game Play:
- Have the student write a different action verb on at least ten index cards. Mix them up and put them in a pile, face down.
- Have the student draw a card and act out the verb.
- The teacher must guess the verb.
- Take turns being the actor until all the students and the teacher have had a turn and/or all the cards are used.

Game Variations:
- Set a timer when the actor begins. Track how fast the player can guess the verb. Work to beat the quickest time.
- Divide players into teams. When it is their turn, the team picks a teammate to be the actor.
- Have students write down a different adverb on the same number of verb cards created for this game. Encourage students to pick adverbs that end in -ly as well as some that do not. Follow the game play rules, except the student must draw a verb card and an adverb card. The teacher must then guess the adverb and the verb.

Possessive Nouns Slap Jack!

Focus: Possessive Nouns, Proper Nouns, Visual Processing

Number of Players

- Two or more

Game Play:

- Ask students to write nouns on note cards. Students should write at least 20 regular nouns. Then they should write at least 10 possessive nouns. Up to 52 cards may be created, with many more regular nouns than possessive nouns.

- Mix the cards up, then deal the cards clockwise, face down, until all the cards have been passed out. The players may not look at their cards.

- The player to the left of the dealer flips over one card, placing it in a pile in the middle of the table. This continues around the table, each person laying down a card on top of the pile in the middle of the table.

- The first player to slap their hand down on a possessive noun takes the possessive noun card and all the cards in the pile underneath it. They shuffle their new cards within the stack of cards they were dealt and place them face down in front of them.

- If a player slaps a noun that is not a possessive noun, they must give one card, face down, from their pile to the player who laid down the card.

- When the player has no more cards to turn over, they remain in the game until the next possessive noun is turned over. If they fail to win that pile, they are out of the game. The game continues until only one player has cards and wins the game.

Game Variations:

- When the player slaps a possessive noun card, they must use the possessive noun in a sentence to win the pile.

- Create at least ten cards with proper nouns and replace the possessive noun cards. Players then watch for proper nouns to slap.

Fun with Sentences Drawing Game

Focus:
- Subject, Predicate, Sentences, Creativity, Hand-Eye Coordination

Number of Players:
- Two or more

Game Play:
- Ask students to make two stacks of cards. Each stack should each have at least eight cards, equal in number. On the back side of the cards in one stack, write the word "Subject." Write "Predicate" on the back of the second stack.
- Ask the student to write sentences, except they will write the Subject part on one card and the Predicate part on the other.
- Shuffle the Subject stack, then shuffle the Predicate stack.
- The first player takes a card from each stack. The player must draw the sentence for the other players to guess.

Game Variations:
- Set a timer when the player begins to draw. Track how fast the player can guess the sentence. Work to beat the quickest time.
- Divide players into teams. When it is their turn, the team picks a teammate to draw the sentence.

State of Being Verb Story Game

Focus:
- State of Being Verbs, Memory, Creativity

Number of Players:
- Two or more

Game Play:
- Have the student write each state of being verb on index cards for a total of eight cards. Mix up the cards and lay the cards face down in a stack.
- The first player draws a card and starts off the story using the state of being verb on the card they drew. For example, if they drew the verb "are" they could say, "My family and neighbors are going to the zoo." (More than one sentence may be used if needed to set up the story and to use the verb correctly.)
- The next player draws a card and continues the story using the state of being verb they drew. The game ends when all the cards are used. The cards may be reshuffled and the game continued for as long as the game remains fun.

Bonus Challenge:
- Players can retell all the story parts before adding to the story.

Game Variation:
- Mix into the stack the Action Verb cards created for Charades.

Don't Make Me Laugh Word Game

Focus:
- Word Usage, Creativity

Number of Players:
- Two or more

Game Play:
- Ask students to make cards of the words they are learning to use such as a-an, see-saw-seen. Write all forms of each set of words on the card. If you use the list below, you should have 14 cards.
- Shuffle the cards and place them in a stack, face down. The first player draws a card. The player must say one or more sentences using all the words on the card correctly, with the intent of making the next player laugh. If the player fails to make the next player laugh, they must draw a new card and try again. Continue to play until all the cards are used. The stack may be reshuffled and the game continued as long as it remains fun.

Game Variations:
- Set a timer when the player draws the card. Track how fast the player takes to make the next player laugh. Work to beat the quickest time.
- Divide players into teams. When it is their turn, the team picks a teammate to be the player who tries to make the opposing team laugh.
- Add more state of being verbs, synonyms, antonyms, homophones, and/or homonyms to the stack of cards.

Word list:

is, am, are	has, have, had	this, that, these, those
to, too, two	see, saw, seen	sit, set
there, their, they're	eat, ate, eaten	it's, its
a, an, the	go, went, gone	who's, whose
be, been, being	most, almost	

Language Level 3 – Activities and Games

Synonym Story Game (Antonyms, Homophones, Homonyms)

Focus:
- Synonyms, Antonyms, Homophones, Homonyms, Auditory Perception, Memory, Creativity

Number of Players:
- Two or more

Game Play:
- Similar to the State of Being Verb Story Game, but with a twist. Students may either create a list of words to draw from or choose words as the game is played.
- The first player either draws a card or chooses a word. The next player must use a synonym of that word to start off the story.
- The player then draws a card or says a word for the next player. The next player then continues the story using a synonym of the word. The game continues until every player has had a turn or as long as the game is fun.

Bonus Challenge:
- Players can retell all the story parts before adding to the story.

Game Variations:
- Players must use the antonym of the word for their story.
- Players must use a homophone in their story. This works best when cards are used. Have the student write a homophone on at least eight cards. The player whose turn it is to tell the next part of the story must use the homophone twice, using the two different meanings.
- Players must use a homonym in their story. This works best when cards are used. Have the student write homonyms (all forms of the word — him/hymn, they're/their/there, etc.) on at least eight cards. The player whose turn it is to tell the next part of the story must use all the homonyms. For example, if the homonym "him/hymn" is selected, the player might say, "I heard him sing a hymn."

Don't Make Me Laugh Simile Game

Focus: Similes, Comparison using -er, -est

Number of Players

- Two or more

Game Play:

- Ask students to write nouns on note cards. Students should write at least 20 nouns.
- Create two piles of cards, face down.
- The first player draws one card from each pile.
- The player must use a simile to tell how the two nouns on the cards are alike using the word *as* or *like*. For example, if "dog" and "car" are the nouns, the player might say, "The dog is as fast as a car." The player should try to make the next player laugh. If the player fails to make the next player laugh, another set of cards is drawn and the player tries again. Continue to play until all the cards are used. The stacks may be shuffled, and the game continued as long as it remains fun.

Game Variation:

- Have the student compare the two nouns using words ending in *-er* or *-est*. Examples: "The dog is faster than the car." "The car is fast, but the dog is the fastest."

Paragraph Sandwich Game

Focus: Paragraphs, Memory, Creativity

Number of Players

- Two or more

Game Play:

- Remind students that writing a paragraph is like making a sandwich. Use the sandwich image to guide students through the game.
- The player creates a topic sentence.
- The next player says the topic sentence, then adds the first detail sentence.
- The next player says the topic sentence, the first detail sentence, then adds a second detail sentence.
- The next player says the topic sentence, the first detail sentence, the second detail sentence, and adds a third detail sentence.
- The next player says the topic sentence, the first, second, and third detail sentences, then adds the concluding sentence.
- The next player recites the whole paragraph.
- The game can continue again for as long as it remains fun.

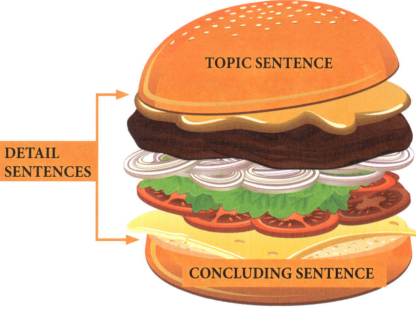

Spelling Practice

The research on how people learn to spell indicates that spelling mastery, in part, comes from spelling words correctly through the practice of writing. Words studied in isolation, in abstract lists, do not carry over from the study to correct use. To help a student learn how to spell a problem word, you can find the word's origins in a dictionary, study the prefixes and suffixes, and practice the basic spelling rules that apply. The spelling word lists on the next few pages can be used to help students know all the words from each lesson through the various spelling practice ideas provided. Then students may mark each word with a check mark to show their spelling word accomplishment.

Some students will need more practice than others when it comes to spelling. We have provided these ideas to help students who need the practice.

Magnetic Letters — Have students use the letters to put together their spelling words for the week.

Memory Game — Write half of the word on one index card and half of the word on the other. Play the Memory Game by having the student search for the other half of the word.

Memory Game — Write the word on one card and the definition on the other. Play the memory game.

Hot Potato — If you have several children, have them sit in a circle and toss around a small object like a bean bag. Play music. Shut the music off at random times (a small sand timer may also be used). Whoever has the "hot potato" when the music turns off must spell a word from their spelling list. (The teacher may choose the word for each student.) If the student spells the word correctly, they stay in the game.

Bingo — Play a game of bingo using spelling words for each square.

Spelling Bee — Hold a weekly spelling bee using the spelling words each student is working on.

One Letter at a Time — Have the student write the first letter of the word. Underneath that, have the student write the next two letters. Underneath the first two letters, have the student write the first three letters of the word. Continue until the entire word is written. Have the students write all the words for the week or just the ones they are having trouble with.

Charades — Play a game of charades using spelling words, except the players must spell the word they are guessing.

Flashcards — Have the student practice using the cards by looking at the word, turning the card over, and either spelling it to themselves, out loud, or by writing the word.

Right Brain Flashcards — Have the student write the word and draw pictures of the word or things that remind them how to spell it. Stickers and other items may be used. Hint: On the back side, the student can draw memory prompts. That side can be used to spell the word without looking at the word itself.

Word Board Games — Use board games that encourage spelling. Have students use their spelling words while playing them.

Internet Word Games — Search the Internet for safe, fun games that encourage spelling skills.

Spelling List

On the following pages are the spelling words from each lesson. You may choose to write out the words below that the student needs additional work on and to share this list with the student. Then you can work on those words together. **Note:** Students may want to put a star next to problem words each time they spell the word correctly in a sentence. Be sure to praise the student's progress as stars are accumulated.

(1) _____   (11) _____

(2) _____   (12) _____

(3) _____   (13) _____

(4) _____   (14) _____

(5) _____   (15) _____

(6) _____   (16) _____

(7) _____   (17) _____

(8) _____   (18) _____

(9) _____   (19) _____

(10) _____   (20) _____

Language Level 3 – Spelling List

(21) _____
(22) _____
(23) _____
(24) _____
(25) _____
(26) _____
(27) _____
(28) _____
(29) _____
(30) _____

(31) _____
(32) _____
(33) _____
(34) _____
(35) _____
(36) _____
(37) _____
(38) _____
(39) _____
(40) _____

Spelling Words

Lesson 1
- ask
- basket
- candy
- check
- damp
- every
- help
- left
- next
- stand

Lesson 2
- admit
- adopt
- doctor
- drink
- lunch
- pond
- slip
- such
- under
- until

Lesson 3
- away
- brain
- game
- nail
- pray
- raise
- sail
- state
- take
- today

Lesson 4
- baby
- breeze
- clean
- easy
- keep
- meal
- need
- seat
- sleep
- theme

Lesson 5
- bike
- child
- dime
- hydrant
- July
- light
- pilot
- quiet
- sigh
- sign

Lesson 6
- alone
- cold
- grow
- hope
- moan
- most
- open
- road
- woke
- yellow

Lesson 7
- grew
- huge
- juice
- music
- newt
- noon
- root
- took
- truth
- tune

Lesson 9
- _____
- _____
- _____
- _____
- _____
- _____
- _____
- _____
- _____
- _____

Lesson 11
- avoid
- choice
- coil
- destroy
- enjoy
- moist
- oyster
- poison
- royal
- voyage

Lesson 8
- about
- done
- eight
- laugh
- much
- myself
- seven
- shall
- start
- today

Lesson 10
- boasting
- cried
- dragged
- hoping
- hopping
- pushed
- saved
- stopped
- trying
- using

Lesson 12
- dirty
- first
- hurt
- lunar
- mayor
- never
- offer
- rural
- shirt
- world

Language Level 3 – Spelling Words

Lesson 13
- begins
- books
- boxes
- catches
- horses
- inches
- keys
- knees
- pinches
- tables

Lesson 14
- babies
- copies
- families
- flies
- knives
- ladies
- leaves
- loaves
- shelves
- thieves

Lesson 15
- cacti
- children
- corn
- deer
- fish
- geese
- mice
- people
- sheep
- women

Lesson 16
- airplane
- anything
- bookcase
- breakfast
- everyone
- hallway
- inside
- keyboard
- rainbow
- sunshine

Lesson 17
- can't
- he's
- I'm
- it'll
- let's
- she'd
- they're
- we've
- won't
- you're

Lesson 18
- _____
- _____
- _____
- _____
- _____
- _____
- _____
- _____
- _____
- _____

Language Level 3 – Spelling Words

Lesson 19
- before
- board
- care
- cure
- dairy
- future
- hair
- mare
- shore
- soar

Lesson 21
- brick
- camp
- check
- inspect
- loft
- mend
- mold
- pond
- pump
- swift

Lesson 23
- can
- duck
- fly
- leaves
- light
- match
- pitcher
- ring
- ruler
- yard

Lesson 20
- play
- plow
- press
- prison
- shape
- shingle
- shut
- thank
- that
- then

Lesson 22
- knows
- meat
- meet
- nose
- pair
- peace
- pear
- piece
- stair
- stare

Lesson 24
- discover
- dislike
- immature
- impolite
- inactive
- intake
- reheat
- return
- undone
- unpack

Lesson 25
- biggest
- carried
- closest
- copied
- directly
- endless
- finally
- healthy
- thirsty
- useless

Lesson 26
- autograph
- biography
- biology
- biopsy
- graph
- microscope
- phone
- photograph
- scope
- symphony

Lesson 27
- _____
- _____
- _____
- _____
- _____
- _____
- _____
- _____
- _____
- _____

Lesson 28
- crept
- feast
- hang
- kept
- prank
- skate
- stink
- strong
- test
- toast

Lesson 29
- batch
- beach
- catch
- cheap
- chew
- ditch
- itch
- peach
- reach
- scratch

Lesson 30
- scrap
- shred
- shrink
- splash
- spray
- spread
- squawk
- stray
- three
- throw

Language Level 3 – Spelling Words

Lesson 31
- cough
- fancy
- father
- fence
- form
- laugh
- orphan
- phrase
- tough
- trophy

Lesson 32
- along
- edge
- engine
- game
- gentle
- germ
- give
- gone
- stage
- sugar

Lesson 33
- castle
- gnaw
- gnat
- knee
- knock
- lamb
- thumb
- wrestle
- wrong
- wrote

Lesson 34
- class
- current
- dress
- fiddle
- follow
- full
- little
- matter
- tall
- wiggle

Lesson 35
- first
- second
- third
- fourth
- fifth
- sixth
- seventh
- eighth
- ninth
- tenth

Lesson 36
- _____
- _____
- _____
- _____
- _____
- _____
- _____
- _____
- _____
- _____

Language Level 3 – Spelling Words

Sight Words

We have provided sight words from previous levels. Please be sure the student can read these words easily. If not, practice them regularly until they are mastered.

Sight words the student has mastered in *Foundations Phonics*:

- a
- all
- an
- and
- are
- as
- at
- be
- but
- by
- can
- did
- for
- from
- get
- had
- has
- have
- he
- his
- how
- I
- if
- is
- it
- my
- no
- not
- of
- on
- or
- out
- see
- she
- so
- than
- that
- the
- them
- then
- they
- this
- to
- was
- we
- what
- when
- who
- will
- you

Language Level 3 – Sight Words

Sight words the student has mastered in *Language Lessons for a Living Education Level 2*:

- always
- around
- because
- been
- before
- best
- both
- buy
- call
- cold
- does
- don't
- fast
- first
- five
- found
- gave
- goes
- green
- its
- made
- many
- off
- or
- pull
- read
- right
- sing
- sit
- sleep
- tell
- their
- these
- those
- upon
- us
- use
- very
- wash
- which
- why
- wish
- work
- would
- write
- your

Sight words the student has mastered in *Language Lessons for a Living Education Level 3*:

- about
- better
- bring
- carry
- clean
- cut
- done
- draw
- drink
- eight
- fall
- far
- full
- got
- grow
- hold
- hot
- hurt
- if
- keep
- laugh
- light
- long
- much
- myself
- never
- only
- own
- pick
- seven
- shall
- show
- six
- small
- start
- ten
- today
- together
- try
- warm

Copywork Practice

(1) The vowels are a, e, i, o, u.

(2) A noun names a person, place, or thing.

(3) A proper noun names a noun and begins with a capital letter.

(4) Singular means one.

(5) Plural means more than one.

(6) A pronoun stands for another noun.

(7) An adjective is a word that describes a person, place, or thing.

(8) An adverb tells about a verb.

(9) A possessive noun shows who or what owns or has something.

(10) A quotation is when you copy exactly what someone has said.

(11) An action verb tells what is happening in a sentence.

(12) Some verbs show a state of being rather than action.

(13) A preposition is a word that links a noun (or pronoun) to another word in the sentence.

(14) Compound words are two words made into one, which gives it a new meaning.

(15) When we write a paragraph, we start with a topic sentence.

We add two or three detail sentences.

We end with a concluding sentence.

(16) Synonyms are two words that mean the same thing.

(17) Antonyms are two words that have opposite meanings.

(18) Homonyms are words that sound the same, mean something different, and are spelled the same.

(19) Homophones are words that sound the same, mean something different, and are spelled differently.

(20) Truth means something that is true or real.

(21) Fiction is a story that is made up or not true.

(22) A simile compare two different things using the words like or as.

(23) The subject is who the sentence is about.

(24) The predicate is what the subject does or is.

(25) There are 24 hours in a day.

(26) There are 365 days in a year.

(27) A contraction is two words that are shortened into one, with an apostrophe in place of the letters that were removed.

(28) A root word is a word to which we add a prefix or suffix.

(29) Initials are the first letters of the first, middle, or last name of a person, followed by a period.

(30) An abbreviation is the shortened form of a word.

(31) Mister is the title of a man.

(32) Miss is the title of an unmarried woman.

(33) Missus is the title of a married woman.

Days of the Week Practice

Sunday = Sun.

Monday = Mon.

Tuesday = Tues.

Wednesday = Wed.

Thursday = Thurs.

Friday = Fri.

Saturday = Sat.

Language Level 3 – Days of the Week Practice

Months of the Year Practice

January = Jan.

February = Feb.

March = Mar.

April = Apr.

May = May

June = June

July = July

August = Aug.

September = Sept.

October = Oct.

November = Nov.

December = Dec.

Ordinal Number Practice

(1) first

(2) second

(3) third

(4) fourth

(5) fifth

(6) sixth

(7) seventh

(8) eighth

(9) ninth

(10) tenth

Contraction Practice

Write the contraction for each set of words.

(1) did not _____

(2) they are _____

(3) you have _____

(4) let us _____

(5) we have _____

(6) are not _____

(7) do not _____

(8) has not _____

(9) you are _____

(10) I am _____

(11) will not _____

(12) is not _____

Titles Practice

Write the abbreviation for each title.

Mister _____   Professor _____

Miss _____   Honorable _____

Missus _____   Senator _____

Doctor _____   President _____

Reverend _____   Captain _____

Detective _____   General _____

Sergeant _____

Representative _____

Calendar Study Sheets

There are 7 days in a week:

Sunday, Monday, Tuesday, Wednesday, Thursday, Friday, Saturday

There are 12 months in a year:

January, February, March, April, May, June, July, August, September, October, November, December

There are 24 hours in a day.

There are 365 days in a year.

Days of the Months Poem

30 days has September,
April, June, and November
All the rest have 31
Except for February
Which has 28
But 29 in a leap year

Seasons of the Year
  Spring = March, April, May (warm)
Summer = June, July, August (hot)
    Fall = September, October, November (cool)
  Winter = December, January, February (cold)

Here is how you write a date:
  January 1, 2022

Grammar Study Sheets

Alphabet

The alphabet is a, b, c, d, e, f, g, h, i, j, k, l, m, n, o, p, q, r, s, t, u, v, w, x, y, z.

Vowels

The vowels are a, e, i, o, u, and sometimes y.

Types of Sentences

The four types of sentences.

Imperative: This type of sentence is a command and ends with a period.

Declarative: This type of sentence is a statement and ends with a period, too.

Exclamatory: This type sentence is an exclamation and has emotion. It ends with an exclamation point.

Interrogative: This means a question. This type of sentence ends with a question mark.

Noun

A noun names a person, place, or thing.

Proper Noun

A proper noun names a noun and begins with a capital letter.

Pronoun

A pronoun stands for another noun: I, you, me, he, him, she, her, it, we, they

Plural Noun

Plural nouns name more than one person, place, or thing.

plural = add -s
ends in s, ss, sh, ch, or x = add -es

vowel + y, add -s	vowel + o, add -s	consonant + o, add -es

piano = pianos   photo = photos

When a word ends in a consonant and the letter y, we make it plural by changing the y to i and then add -es.

Ends in f or fe = change f or fe to v and add -es

| roof = roofs | cliff = cliffs |

Single	Plural	Single	Plural
man	men	goose	geese
woman	women	mouse	mice
child	children	ox	oxen
person	people	octopus	octopi
		cactus	cacti

Single	Plural	Single	Plural
deer	deer	moose	moose
fish	fish	corn	corn
sheep	sheep	seaweed	seaweed

Sentences

A sentence must end in a punctuation mark:

period .   question mark ?   exclamation point !

Language Level 3 – Grammar Study Sheets

Subject — Predicate

Subject tells who or what the sentence is about.

Predicate tells what the subject does or is.

Possessive Noun

A possessive noun shows who or what owns or has something. We make a singular noun possessive by adding an apostrophe and an -s. We make a plural noun that ends in an -s possessive by adding the apostrophe to the end of the word.

Commas

We use a comma when we write a list of things in a sentence.

We use a comma when we address someone.

Action Verbs — State of Being Verbs

Action verbs tell what is happening in a sentence.

State of being verbs show state of being rather than action. They link the subject to the predicate.

The Eight State of Being Verbs:

is am	are was	were be	been being

Conjunctions

Conjunctions are words that join two words or phrases together.

Here are some common conjunctions:

and but or nor for so

Compound Words

Compound words are two words made into one with a new meaning.

Language Level 3 – Grammar Study Sheets

Adjective

An adjective is a word that describes a person, place, or thing.

Adjectives describe: colors, sizes, shapes, tastes, smells, sounds, looks, feels, how many, weather, feelings, behaviors

Contractions

Contractions are two words that are shortened into one, with an apostrophe in place of the missing letters.

Common Contractions

aren't = are not
didn't = did not
don't = do not
hasn't = has not
isn't = is not
can't = can not
won't = will not

you're = you are
they're = they are
you've = you have
we've = we have
I'm = I am
let's = let us

Adverb

Adverbs tell about a verb. An adverb often ends in -ly and describes how, when, where, or how often a verb happens.

There are many adverbs. Here is a list of examples to study:

How	When	Where	How Often
gently	early	above	daily
quickly	now	inside	never
quietly	soon	here	often
sadly	tomorrow	outside	usually
safely	yesterday	upstairs	yearly

Quotation

A quotation is when you copy exactly what someone has said.

- Remember to use a comma before the quote.
- Remember to use a capital letter to start the first word of the quote.
- Remember to use quotation marks before and after the quote.

Language Level 3 – Grammar Study Sheets

Preposition

A preposition is a word that links a noun (or pronoun) to another word in the sentence. It shows a relationship between a noun and another word. A prepositional phrase begins with a preposition and ends with a noun. Prepositions show location. These are common prepositions:

above	on	inside	in
below	off	outside	to
over	before	with	into
under	after	through	by

Articles

a + consonant
an + vowel
the + specific noun

Sentence Combining

We can make our writing better by combining sentences.

Language Level 3 – Grammar Study Sheets

Paragraph

A paragraph is a group of sentences about a specific idea or topic. A paragraph should:

- Start on a new line with an indent.
- Include at least four sentences.
- Start with a topic sentence.
- Include 2-3 sentences that give details about the topic.
- End with a concluding sentence. This sentence ends the paragraph by saying the topic in another way.

Interjections

Interjections are words that expresses emotion or feelings. Often, they are found at the beginning of a sentence and are followed by an exclamation point.

Synonyms — Antonyms

Synonyms are two words that mean the same thing.

Antonyms are two words that have opposite meanings.

Homophones — Homonyms

Homophones are words that sound the same, mean something different, and are spelled differently.

Homonyms are words that sound the same, mean something different, and are spelled the same.

Homophones:	Homonyms:
• Sound the same • Different meanings • Spelled differently	• Sound the same • Different meanings • Spelled the same
Example: male — mail	Example: glasses — glasses

Truth/Fiction

> Truth means something that is true or real. Fiction is a story that is made up or not true.

Simile

> A simile compares two different things using the words *like* or *as*.

To — Too — Two

| to = direction | too = also or a lot | two = number |

There — Their — They're

> there = a place
> their = belonging to others
> they're = a contraction that means "they are"

Is — Am — Are

> is = one, present tense
> am = one, present tense
> are = more than one, present tense

Be — Been — Being

The verb *be* refers to the present.	The verb *been* refers to the past.	The verb *being* refers to the past and needs a helping verb.
I will be back soon.	I have been gone a while.	I am being chased by a dog.

Has — Have — Had

The helping verbs *has* and *have* are in the present and show there is possession.

have	has
I have they have	he has she has
you have we have	it has

When we are talking about something in the past, we use the word *had.*

Language Level 3 – Grammar Study Sheets

See — Saw — Seen

The verb *see* refers to the present.	The verb *saw* refers to the past.	The verb *seen* refers to the past and needs a helping verb.
I see.	I saw.	I have seen.

Eat — Ate — Eaten

The verb *eat* refers to the present.	The verb *ate* refers to the past.	The verb *eaten* refers to the past and needs a helping verb.
I eat.	I ate.	I have eaten.

Go — Went — Gone

The verb *go* refers to the present.	The verb *went* refers to the past.	The verb *gone* refers to the past. It needs a helping verb.
I go.	I went.	I have gone.

Most — Almost

most = the largest amount	almost = nearly

This — That — These — Those

	Near	Far
Singular	this	that
Plural	these	those

Sit — Set

sit = rest in an upright position	set = place an object
I like to sit in my new chair.	I set my lunch on the table.

It's — Its

it's = it is	its = possession (and breaks the rules)
It's going to be a great day.	Give the dog its bone.

Whose — Who's

who's = who is	whose = possession (and breaks the rules)

Root Word

Root words are the words we add a suffix or a prefix to.

Suffix -ed, -ing

Root word ends with a silent e = drop the e before adding the suffix

Root word has one syllable, one short vowel, and ends with one consonant = double the consonant then add -ed or -ing.

kick : kicked, kicking
bake : baked, baking
stop : stopped, stopping

Prefix un-, re-, in-, im-, dis-, pre-, tele-

un- means not
re- means again
in- means not, in, or on
im- means not, in, or on
  (use im- for words that begin with b, m, and p)
dis- means not or opposite of
pre- means before
tele- means far or distant

Initials

Initials are the first letter of the first, middle, or last name of a person.

Titles

Mister is the title of a man.
Miss is the title of an unmarried woman.
Missus is the title of a married woman.

We can abbreviate these titles.

Mister = Mr.
Miss = Ms.
Missus = Mrs.

We can abbreviate other titles.

Doctor = Dr.
Reverend = Rev.
Detective = Det.
Professor = Prof.

We can abbreviate titles related to our government.

Honorable = Hon.
Senator = Sen.
Representative = Rep.
President = Pres.

We can abbreviate titles related to our military.

Captain = Capt.
General = Gen.
Sergeant = Sgt.

Answer Keys

Answers for the numbered problems are provided here with the exception of the Narration Practice questions.

Language Lessons for a Living Education Level 3 — Worksheet Answer Keys

Answers are given for numbered problems on the worksheets.

Lesson 1; Exercise 2; Day 2

1. The (20, 8, 5) quick (17, 21, 9, 3, 11) brown (2, 18, 15, 23, 14) fox (6, 15, 24) jumps (10, 21, 13, 16, 19) over (15, 22, 5, 18) the (20, 8, 5) lazy (12, 1, 26, 25) dog (4, 15, 7)
2. t, h, e, o, u, r
3. o

Lesson 1; Exercise 3; Day 3

1. What are the feasts in the Bible?
2. Mr. Lopez is our teacher.
3. I can't wait to eat a donut!

Lesson 1; Exercise 5; Day 5

1. Micah needed help to reach the sweet candy.
2. He will ask if he can put the pretty flowers in the basket.
3. Claire's shirt was damp after she left it in the rain.
4. Claire and Micah will stand next to each other.
5. Micah and Claire check every answer to make sure they are right.

Lesson 2; Exercise 2; Day 7

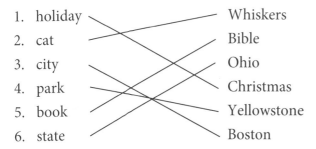

1. holiday
2. cat
3. city
4. park
5. book
6. state

Whiskers
Bible
Ohio
Christmas
Yellowstone
Boston

Lesson 2; Exercise 3; Day 8

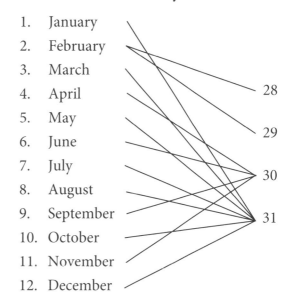

1. January
2. February
3. March
4. April
5. May
6. June
7. July
8. August
9. September
10. October
11. November
12. December

28
29
30
31

Lesson 2; Exercise 5; Day 10

1. drink
2. doctor
3. lunch
4. adopt
5. under
6. slip
7. admit
8. until
9. such
10. pond

Lesson 3; Exercise 2; Day 12

1. Mr. Lopez started the class. He
2. Claire read her Bible. She
3. Micah and Claire were late for class. They
4. I will give you an apple.
5. He will say a prayer before lunch.
6. Hand me the cup.
7. Pass the plates to them.
8. They will enjoy the meal.
9. We are full.
10. She sent us to wash the dishes.

Lesson 3; Exercise 5; Day 15

1. away
2. brain
3. game
4. nail
5. pray
6. raise
7. sail
8. state
9. take
10. today

Lesson 4; Exercise 1; Day 16

Number 4 and 11 are identical.

Lesson 4; Exercise 2; Day 17

1. buses
2. orphans
3. churches
4. boxes
5. smiles
6. bushes
7. hands
8. messes

Lesson 4; Exercise 3; Day 18

1. red
2. blue
3. yellow

Lesson 4; Exercise 5; Day 20

V	S	U	X	M	B	I	U	M	Q	S	T
H	L	Q	O	E	N	R	N	Q	X	E	H
S	E	T	W	A	E	N	B	Z	C	A	E
K	E	E	P	L	E	H	A	U	S	T	M
U	P	C	N	R	D	G	B	H	P	Q	E
M	T	E	A	S	Y	V	Y	O	O	I	Y
G	O	N	T	S	B	R	E	E	Z	E	A
B	T	C	L	E	A	N	B	R	S	L	I
M	E	J	A	Z	K	L	E	S	P	D	C

Lesson 5; Exercise 1; Day 21

1. jump toss **ball** run
2. horse cow goat **lion**
3. **shoe** puzzle frisbee ball
4. **flower** rose tulip peony

Lesson 5; Exercise 2; Day 22

1. toys
2. tornadoes
3. zoos
4. tomatoes
5. patios
6. monkeys

Lesson 5; Exercise 3; Day 23

1. IN Why did the priest blow the shofar?
2. D I like apples slices dipped in honey.
3. E Stop that dog!
4. IM Bring me that book.
5. Oops! I dropped the plate.
6. Oh, were you in line?
7. Hey! Don't touch the hot stove.

Lesson 6; Exercise 2; Day 27

1. city = cities
2. leaf = leaves
3. country = countries
4. knife = knives

Lesson 6; Exercise 3; Day 28

1. I am going to read about the Sabbath, Micah.
2. Claire, did you memorize the verse?
3. What, God, did you want us to remember?

Lesson 6; Exercise 5; Day 30
1. grow
2. road
3. moan
4. cold
5. hope
6. alone
7. woke
8. most
9. yellow
10. open

Lesson 7; Exercise 2; Day 32
1. cactus = catci
2. child = children
3. corn = corn
4. deer = deer
5. fish = fish
6. goose = geese
7. man = men
8. moose = moose
9. mouse = mice
10. octopus = octopi
11. ox = oxen
12. person = people
13. seaweed = seaweed
14. sheep = sheep
15. woman = women

Lesson 7; Exercise 3; Day 33
1. John Quincy Adams = J. Q. A.
2. William Howard Taft = W. H. T.
3. Mister — Mr.
4. Miss — Ms.
5. Missus — Mrs.

6. Doctor — Dr.
7. Reverend — Rev.
8. Detective — Det.
9. Professor — Prof.
10. Honorable — Hon.
11. Senator — Sen.
12. Representative — Rep.
13. President — Pres.
14. Captain — Capt.
15. General — Gen.
16. Sergeant — Sgt.

Lesson 8; Exercise 1; Day 36
1. The fox is asleep.   The fox is hungry.
   The fox is thirsty.   The fox is happy.

Lesson 8; Exercise 2; Day 37
1. The mouse lost its cheese.
2. It's under the couch.
3. The dog's bone was heavy.
4. The dogs' bowls were the same.
5. The dogs were playing.

Lesson 8; Exercise 3; Day 38
1. The cat caught a mouse.
2. The fox played in the field.

Lesson 8; Exercise 5; Day 40
1. about
2. done
3. eight
4. laugh
5. much
6. myself
7. seven
8. shall
9. start
10. today

Lesson 9; Exercise 2; Day 42

1. a b c d e f g h i j k l m n o p q r s t u v w x y z
2. a b c d e f g h i j k l m n o p q r s t u v w x y z
3. holiday — Fido
4. dog — Bible
5. city — Kentucky
6. park — Christmas
7. book — Yellowstone
8. state — Cleveland
9. He will say a prayer before lunch.
10. Hand me the cup.
11. They will enjoy the meal.
12. We are full.
13. church = churches
14. toy = toys
15. city = cities
16. leaf = leaves
17. child = children
18. goose = geese
19. person = people
20. deer = deer
21. man = men
22. Answers will vary.
23. The mouse lost its cheese.
24. It's under the couch.
25. Answers will vary.

Lesson 9; Exercise 3; Day 43

1. Answers will vary.
2. Sunday, Monday, Tuesday, Wednesday, Thursday, Friday, Saturday
3. January, February, March, April, May, June, July, August, September, October, November, December

4. January
5. February
6. March
7. April
8. May
9. June
10. July
11. August
12. September
13. October
14. November
15. December

(matching to 28, 29, 30, 31)

16. IN Why did the priest blow the shofar?
17. D I like apple slices dipped in honey.
18. E Stop that dog!
19. IM Bring me that book.
20. Answers will vary.
21. Answers will vary
22. Answers will vary.
23. Mister = Mr.
24. Missus = Mrs.
25. The cat caught a mouse.

Lesson 10; Exercise 1; Day 46

1. West
2. North
3. East
4. South
5. South
6. Black car
7. Red car
8. Farm
9. West
10. East

Lesson 10; Exercise 2; Day 47

1. Claire runs to class.
2. Claire ran to class.

3. Mom **called** Claire for lunch.
4. Path number 2

Lesson 10; Exercise 3; Day 48

1. Claire **and** Micah were thankful.
2. I love pie, **but** I am full.
3. You can either have apples **or** grapes.
4. I would like apples **and** grapes.
5. I want apples, **but** I like grapes too.
6. I do not like peaches, **nor** do I like kiwi fruit.
7. I put on my shoes, **so** I could go outside.
8. My mom and dad love me very much.

Lesson 11; Exercise 2; Day 52

1. He **is** a nice boy.
2. I **am** late for work.
3. We **are** going to church.
4. Micah and Claire **were** thankful.
5. Mr. Lopez **was** giving away Bibles.
6. Ruth was **being** kind to Naomi.
7. Ruth and Naomi have **been** on a long trip.
8. They will **be** in Israel soon.
9.
```
T  C  L  L  P  U  Z  P  J  J
T  Y  B  E  E  N  J  C  N  N
U  W  Y  M  X  P  Y  B  E  G
Y  B  E  I  N  G  V  Z  W  W
R  N  T  G  Q  R  H  Z  B  R
W  I  S  G  I  S  B  K  A  M
G  A  R  E  G  Q  J  Z  G  Q
R  B  A  N  A  W  E  R  E  X
F  T  A  I  V  A  O  V  R  C
D  M  I  L  K  S  I  Z  Z  B
```

Lesson 11; Exercise 3; Day 53

1. cowboy
2. toothbrush
3. cornbread
4. football
5. horseshoe
6. firefly

Lesson 12; Exercise 2; Day 57

1. The <u>gray</u> **cat** jumped onto the <u>large</u> **chair**.
2. The <u>small</u>, <u>round</u> **balloon** flew up into the <u>blue</u> **sky**.
3. The <u>sour</u> **candy** is in the bowl.
4. The <u>loud</u> **thunder** shook our house.
5. The <u>stinky</u> **skunk** ran under the porch.
6. The <u>five soft</u> **bunnies** ran into the hole.
7. The <u>pretty</u> **bird** sang <u>two</u> **songs**.
8. The <u>rainy</u> **day** kept the <u>sad</u> **dog** inside.
9. The slow **slug** moved along the leaf.

Lesson 12; Exercise 3; Day 58

1. could've — could have
2. doesn't — does not
3. wasn't — was not
4. they'll — they will
5. how's — how is
6. I've — I have
7. we'd — we would
8. must've — must have
9. did not = **didn't**
10. they are = **they're**
11. you have = **you've**
12. let us = **let's**
13. we have = **we've**
14. are not = **aren't**
15. do not = **don't**
16. has not = **hasn't**
17. you are = **you're**
18. I am = **I'm**
19. will not = **won't**
20. is not = **isn't**

Lesson 12; Exercise 5; Day 60

1. trshi = shirt

2. rrlau = rural
3. rlnau = lunar
4. frfeo = offer
5. tsfri = first
6. rnvee = never
7. thru = hurt
8. rmyao = mayor
9. yrdti = dirty
10. dlrwo = world

Lesson 13; Exercise 1; Day 61

1. The cat ran into a tree.
   She is high up but can still see.
2. I wonder what is in the box.
   Could it be a pair of socks.
3. I went swimming in a pool.
   I was hot but now I'm cool.
4. "Read a book" my mom said.
   So I took a book to read in bed.

Lesson 13; Exercise 3; Day 63

1. Mom said, "Use kind words with each other."
2. Claire asked, "How is showing mercy like planting seeds?"
3. Mr. Lopez explained, "Small things can turn into big things."
4. Micah yelled, "Watch out for the car!"

Lesson 13; Exercise 5; Day 65

1. My ruler measures in inches.
2. Dad put his keys on the table.
3. The wood worker built two new tables.
4. We packed many boxes when we moved.
5. The book begins with a sad story.
6. They rode their horses in the field.
7. He got down on his knees to pray.
8. Ouch! This chair pinches me when I sit.
9. Please take the books back to the library.
10. The dog always catches the ball.

Lesson 14; Exercise 2; Day 67

1. The bird flew through the window.
2. Claire walked by the cat.
3. Micah played with the dog.
4. The ball went over the roof.

Lesson 14; Exercise 3; Day 68

1. Passport to the World is a fun book to read.
2. I was in a play called The Story of Ruth.
3. Have you watched Extreme Caving by Buddy Davis?
4. i dig dinosaurs = I Dig Dinosaurs
5. whale of a story = Whale of a Story
6. a special door = A Special Door
7. pilgrim's progress = Pilgrim's Progress
8. the life of moses = The Life of Moses

Lesson 15; Exercise 2; Day 72

1. My family and I went to two parks with our two friends before we went to two zoos to see too many zebras to count and an elephant, too.

Lesson 15; Exercise 3; Day 73

1. door
2. dove
3. drain
4. duck
5. dune
6. dust

Lesson 15; Exercise 5; Day 75

1.
```
Y C H I L D R E N I P M
D E E R F K O V W P C J
C J I R Y B A P T M A W
O R A G Y S R E P A C O
R R N S Z N P O G X T M
N D X R W G U P E M I E
Q M I R Q U Q L E I M N
Y O K J C Y W E S C E Z
K Q X B K Z F K E E S X
T S H E E P Q Q F I S H
```

Lesson 16; Exercise 1; Day 76

1. cat
2. ball
3. tree
4. run
5. yell
6. jump
7. sweet
8. pretty
9. fast

Lesson 16; Exercise 2; Day 77

1. They're going on a field trip.
2. I love their garden.
3. The cat ran over there.

Lesson 16; Exercise 3; Day 78

1. ~~She has green.~~
2. I love my parrot.
3. ~~Name is Polly.~~
4. She eats seeds.
5. IN What is the true meaning of Christmas?
6. D Jesus came to the earth as a baby.
7. E Don't fall off the stage!
8. IM Go get the song list.
9. Jin and Ava practiced for the play.
10. Ava and her family prayed and read the Bible.

Lesson 17; Exercise 1; Day 81

1. The Lord is my shepherd, — I shall not want.
2. He makes me lie down in green pastures; — He leads me beside quiet waters.
3. He restores my soul; — He guides me in the paths of righteousness For His name's sake.
4. Even though I walk through the valley of the shadow of death, — I fear no evil, for You are with me; Your rod and Your staff, they comfort me.
5. You prepare a table before me in the presence of my enemies; — You have anointed my head with oil; My cup overflows.
6. Surely goodness and lovingkindness will follow me all the days of my life, — And I will dwell in the house of the Lord forever.

Lesson 17; Exercise 2; Day 82

1. Jin was in a (or the) Christmas play at church.
2. Micah gave the (or a) cookie to Ava.
3. Claire put on an apron.

Lesson 17; Exercise 5; Day 85

1. they are = they're
2. he is = he's
3. you are = you're
4. can not = can't
5. we have = we've
6. it will = it'll
7. she would = she'd
8. I am = I'm
9. let us = let's
10. will not = won't

Lesson 18; Exercise 1; Day 86
1. F It is snowing.
2. O The birds are hungry.
3. F The birds are sitting on a branch.
4. O The birds want to fly south.

Lesson 18; Exercise 2; Day 87
1. Claire runs to class. present tense
2. Claire ran to class. past tense
3. He is a nice boy.
4. I am late for work.
5. We are going to church.
6. Micah and Claire were thankful.
7. Mr. Lopez was giving away Bibles.
8. Ruth was being kind to Naomi.
9. Ruth and Naomi have been on a long trip.
10. They will be in Israel soon.
11. The stinky skunk ran under the porch.
12. The slow slug moved along the leaf.
13. The cat climbed the tree quickly.
14. The girl sang a song yesterday.
15. Claire walked by the cat.
16. The ball went over the roof.
17. to — number
18. too — also or a lot
19. two — direction
20. there — belonging to others
21. their — they are
22. they're — a place
23. Jin was in a (or the) Christmas play at church.
24. Micah gave the (or a) cookie to Ava.
25. Claire put on an apron.

Lesson 18; Exercise 3; Day 88
1. I love pie, but I am full.
2. You can have apples and grapes.
3. tooth — boy
4. cow — ball
5. foot — brush
6. did not = didn't
7. they are = they're
8. Mom said, "Use kind words with each other."
9. Passport to the World is a fun book to read.
10. door
11. duck
12. I love my parrot.
13. ~~Name is Polly.~~
14. Jin and Ava practiced for the play.
15. Ava and her family prayed and read the Bible.
16. A paragraph is like a sandwich. — First Detail Sentence
17. You start with a sentence, which is the first piece of bread. — Topic Sentence
18. You add detail sentences for the meat, cheese, and mustard. — Concluding Sentence
19. Then you write an ending sentence for the bottom piece of bread. — Third Detail Sentence
20. I like to make paragraph sandwiches! — Second Detail Sentence
21. IN What is the true meaning of Christmas?
22. IM Jesus came to the earth as a baby.
23. E Don't fall off the stage!
24. D Go get the song list.
25. Answers will vary.

Lesson 18; Exercise 5; Day 90
1. play = 9
2. lazy = 16
3. church = 16

Language Level 3 — Answer Keys

4. cookies = 13
5. singing = 9
6. Christmas = 14
7. play, singing

Lesson 19; Exercise 2; Day 92

1. He has a cute dog.
2. They have fun playing catch.
3.

Lesson 19; Exercise 3; Day 93

1. Claire waved at Ava and Micah.
2. Micah ran to Claire quickly.
3. Ave and Claire met Jin.
4. A paragraph is like a sandwich. — Topic Sentence
5. You start with a sentence, which is the first piece of bread. — First Detail Sentence
6. You add detail sentences for the meat, cheese, and mustard. — Second Detail Sentence / Third Detail Sentence
7. Then you write an ending sentence for the bottom piece of bread. — Concluding Sentence
8. I like to make paragraph sandwiches!

Lesson 19; Exercise 5; Day 95

1. care or mare or soar or cure
2. mare or care or soar or cure
3. before or future
4. soar or care or mare or cure
5. hair
6. board
7. dairy
8. shore
9. cure or care or mare or soar
10. future or before

Lesson 20; Exercise 2; Day 97

1. Claire and Ava have brushed the cat.
2. Jin has walked the dog.

Lesson 20; Exercise 3; Day 98

1. close — pass
2. happy — sad
3. give — take
4. rest — jog
5. run — relax
6. open — shut
7. happy — glad
8. give — near
9. rest — work
10. run — walk

Lesson 20; Exercise 5; Day 100

1. The opposite of open. shut
2. How to be grateful. thank
3. A place you do not want to be. prison
4. Something kids like to do. play
5. The outline of something. shape
6. A farmer does this to a field. plow
7. This can be found on the top of a house. shingle
8. Not this but that.

9. First this, then that.
10. To push down on something. press

Lesson 21; Exercise 1; Day 101
1. Market
2. Circus
3. North
4. Tire Center

Lesson 21; Exercise 2; Day 102
1. I have seen Micah and Jin work on their memory verse.
2. I saw Ava write down her Bible verse yesterday.
3. I see Claire every Sunday.
4. I saw two children reading to animals in the forest. Can you see them too? I have never seen anything like it!

Lesson 21; Exercise 3; Day 103

1. homophones — sound the same, different meanings, different spelling
2. homonyms — same spelling, different meanings

Lesson 22; Exercise 1; Day 106
1. Whenever I am feeling down,
   My big brown dog comes around.
2. He likes to go outside to run.
   I throw him a ball. It's lots of fun.
3. He lays by my bed as I go to sleep.
   I whisper to him as I count some sheep.
4. My dog is a very good friend,
   Each day is so fun I don't like it to end.

Lesson 22; Exercise 2; Day 107
1. I have ____ lunch already. — eaten
2. I ____ my last banana earlier. — ate
3. I ____ dinner every day. — eat

Lesson 22; Exercise 3; Day 108
1. do: = undo
2. fair: = unfair
3. move: = remove
4. turn: = return

Lesson 22; Exercise 5; Day 110
1. My nose knows when something is stinky.
2. The pear sat on a pair of plates.
3. We will meet at the grill to cook meat.
4. Before I step on the stair I will stare at it to make sure I don't trip.
5. I have peace about the piece of pie that fell off my plate.

Lesson 23; Exercise 1; Day 111
1. The panda jumped up and down.
2. The panda ate bamboo.
3. The panda was old.
4. The panda laid down at the end of a long day.
5. She ran through the woods. She ate grapes. She swam in the river.
6. They fished before they ate lunch.
7. He thought about the fun he had that day. He surprised his mom with flowers he picked himself. Then he swam with his brother and sister all day.
8. The panda didn't like to eat bamboo. He like to eat apples. He ate lettuce instead.
9. The panda ran through the house as fast as he could.
10. The panda was tired but happy.
11. The panda went out and fixed the car.
12. The panda made an apple pie.

Lesson 23; Exercise 2; Day 112
1. I almost finished my lunch.
2. I have the most to eat.
3. I sit at the table.
4. I set my cup on the table.

5. I have gone to that playground many times.
6. I went to the store yesterday.
7. I go get the mail every day.

Lesson 23; Exercise 3; Day 113

1. port: import
2. take: intake
3. like: dislike
4. trust: distrust
5. test: pretest
6. made: premade
7. phone: telephone
8. vision: television

Lesson 23; Exercise 5; Day 115

1. hmtca = match
2. dyra = yard
3. vsleea = leaves
4. tlhgi = light
5. yfl = fly
6. grni = ring
7. rrleu = ruler
8. rphtcei = pitcher
9. kdcu = duck
10. nca = can

Lesson 24; Exercise 2; Day 117

1. I want that book.
2. Those are my pencils.

Lesson 24; Exercise 3; Day 118

1. bake: baked baking
2. stop: stopped stopping
3. add: added adding
4. taste: tasted tasting
5. rip: ripped ripping
6. wished
7. undone
8. resell

9. playing

Lesson 24; Exercise 5; Day 120

1. N F Z Z F Q N T K E A N
    G U D I S L I K E C B R
    D N B J N C O N O N F I
    I P X W D I N T A K E M
    Z A O C R E T U R N R P
    L C P E R E H E A T A O
    L K I N A C T I V E S L
    H D D I S C O V E R N I
    I I M M A T U R E W G T
    H B O U N D O N E L E E

Lesson 25; Exercise 1; Day 121

1. fiction
2. a fox who could fly

Lesson 25; Exercise 2; Day 122

1. The dog buried its bone.
2. It's sunny outside.
3. Who's coming to the picnic?
4. Whose dog is this?
5. blue, yellow, red, purple, green

Lesson 26; Exercise 2; Day 127

1. fast: faster fastest
2. slow: slower slowest
3. tame: tamer tamest

Lesson 26; Exercise 5; Day 130

1. photograph
2. symphony
3. microscope
4. biography
5. autograph
6. graph
7. biopsy
8. scope

Language Level 3 —Answer Keys

9. biology
10. phone

Lesson 27; Exercise 1; Day 131

1. socks, shirt, pants, hat
2. Bible, atlas, dictionary, thesaurus
3. apple, crackers, carrot, cheese
4. ball, game, blocks, teddy bear

Lesson 27; Exercise 2; Day 132

1. Micah and Jin ___ said their verses.
2. Claire ___ written a poem.
3. I have ___ the Lord's mercy.
4. I ___ Micah help Jin last week.
5. I can ___ Ava reading her Bible.
6. I will ___ my lunch soon.
7. I have ___ my snack already.
8. I ___ my breakfast early this morning.
9. I will ___ to bed soon.
10. I have ___ to bed early every night.
11. I ___ to bed late last night.
12. I am ___ done reading my book
13. I have ___ of my room clean.
14. ___ your book on the table.
15. ___ down and tell me about your day.
16. I want ___ Bible to read.
17. Do ___ look like my socks?
18. I like ___ apples.
19. Is ___ my pencil?
20. The cat lost ___ toy.
21. Mom, ___ going to rain soon.

has / have / see / seen / saw / eaten / ate / eat / went / go / gone / most / almost / Sit / Set / these / that / this / those / it's / its

22. ___ coming to our house after church?
23. ___ Bible is this?

Whose / Who's

24. fast: faster fastest
25. white: whiter whitest

Lesson 27; Exercise 3; Day 133

1. Jin and Micah studied the verses.
2. close — glad
3. happy — pass
4. give — near
5. close — take
6. happy — shut
7. give — sad
8. homophones — sound the same / different meanings
9. homonyms — same spelling / different spelling

10. add: added adding
11. taste: tasted tasting
12. rip: ripped ripping
13. unless
14. distrust
15. remove
16. premade
17. income
18. telephone
19. Answers will vary.
20. Answers will vary.

Lesson 28; Exercise 2; Day 137

1. Claire loves her cat.
   She loves her cat.
2. Claire and Ava gave the cat food.
   They gave the cat food.

Lesson 28; Exercise 3; Day 138

1. IN Why did the Claire feel sad?
2. D I like going to church.
3. E Stop that car!
4. IM Bring me a Bible.
5. Bring the dirty clothes here, Jin.
6. Micah saw building blocks, a skateboard, and games in Jin's room.
7. Micah, please bring the skateboard here.
8. You, God, are worthy of praise.
9. Wow! God is good.
10. Oh, did you finish your math?

Lesson 29; Exercise 2; Day 142

1. buses
2. pianos
3. churches
4. boxes
5. bushes
6. photos
7. hands
8. messes
9. radios
10. tomatoes
11. city = cities
12. wolf = wolves
13. roof = roofs
14. country = countries
15. cliff = cliffs
16. knife = knives

17. man — people
18. woman — men
19. child — women
20. person — children

21. goose — geese
22. mouse — mice
23. ox — oxen
24. cactus — cacti

25. deer — deer
26. fish — fish
27. sheep — sheep
28. moose — moose

29. corn — corn
30. seaweed — seaweed
31. octopus — octopi

Lesson 29; Exercise 3; Day 143

1. <u>The girls</u> ate their lunch.
2. <u>The cat</u> ran fast.
3. <u>The corn</u> tasted good.
4. <u>Dad and I</u> saved the cat.
5. I love green beans, **but** I am full.
6. You can either have potatoes **or** squash.
7. I would like peas **and** carrots.
8. I want okra, **but** I like asparagus too.
9. I do not like sweet potatoes, **nor** do I like cucumbers.
10. I ate my dinner, **so** I could go outside.
11. I love to work on math **and** spelling.

Crossword

1. (across) bee
1. (down) butterfly
2. strawberry
3. fish
4. leaf
5. lizard
6. hive
7. flower
8. mushroom
9. (across) stone
9. (down) stump

Language Level 3 —Answer Keys 407

10. ladybug
11. mouse
12. grass
13. cloud
Answer: NATURE

Lesson 30; Exercise 1; Day 146

1. I love to fly!
2. Hitting the ground hurts!
3. I like to take naps.
4. I had a dream I could fly.

Lesson 30; Exercise 2; Day 147

1. toys'
2. dog's
3. cats'
4. chick's
5. The dog lost its toy.
6. It's under the couch.
7. The bird flew into the tree.
8. Claire walked by the garden.
9. Ava played with Claire's cat.
10. The ball went over the fence.

Lesson 30; Exercise 3; Day 148

1. Mom said, "Be nice to each other."
2. Claire asked, "How can we show mercy?"
3. Mr. Lopez said, "Jesus was the Passover Lamb."
4. Ava said, "I want my life to start new."

Lesson 30; Exercise 5; Day 150

1. Do this with a ball. throw
2. A cat or dog without a home. stray
3. Do this to butter on bread. spread
4. To make smaller. shrink
5. Loud sound a bird can make. squawk
6. Water can do this when it comes out of a hose. spray
7. To tear into a lot pieces. shred

8. A small piece of paper. scrap
9. A number. three
10. You can do this with water in the pool. splash

Lesson 31; Exercise 1; Day 151

1. If I want to touch a star,
   I would have to travel far.
2. As I dug deep in the ground,
   An old toy I have found.
3. Out in the woods I climb a tree.
   It is so much fun being free.
4. As I look into the creek,
   It is a fish that I seek.

Lesson 31; Exercise 2; Day 152

1. unless
2. remove
3. income
4. distrust
5. premade
6. telephone
7. add: added adding
8. taste: tasted tasting
9. rip: ripped ripping
10. fast: faster fastest
11. tame: tamer tamest
12. base — fly
13. jelly — ball
14. fire — fish

(12 base → fish, 13 jelly → fly, 14 fire → ball)

Lesson 31; Exercise 3; Day 153

1. doesn't — they will
2. they'll — does not
3. how's — how is
4. I've — we would
5. we'd — must have
6. must've — I have

(1 doesn't → does not, 2 they'll → they will, 4 I've → I have, 5 we'd → we would, 6 must've → must have)

7. let us = let's
8. do not = don't

9. you are = you're
10. I am = I'm
11. Mister — the title of an unmarried woman
12. Miss — the title of a man
13. Missus — the title of a married woman

14. Mister — Mrs.
15. Miss — Ms.
16. Missus — Mr.
17. Doctor — Rev.
18. Reverend — Dr.
19. Detective — Prof.
20. Professor — Det.
21. Honorable — Pres.
22. Senator — Hon.
23. Representative — Sen.
24. President — Rep.
25. Captain — Gen.
26. General — Sgt.
27. Sergeant — Capt.

Lesson 31; Exercise 5; Day 155

1. The **orphan** won a **trophy** for being the most **fancy** dressed boy at the party.
2. My **father** put up a **fence** to keep the **tough** cows in the field.
3. Don't **laugh** or **cough** while you write a funny **phrase** on the form.

Lesson 32; Exercise 1; Day 156

1. Is the firehouse on Elm Street or **Oak Street**?
2. Is the church on Oak Street or **Elm Street**?
3. Is my house is on **Walnut Street** or Oak Street?
4. **Market** Street goes north from my house to Grandma's House.
5. **Park** Street goes south from the basketball court to the Art Center.

Lesson 32; Exercise 2; Day 157

1. That ___ a fun game. — is
2. I ___ good at it. — am
3. We ___ playing the game now. — are
4. Ava and Claire ___ here yesterday. — were
5. Micah ___ with Jin. — was
6. Ava and Claire were ___ gentle with the cat. — being
7. Micah has ___ to Jin's house. — been
8. The friends will ___ in Sunday school soon. — be
9. He ___ a cute dog. — has
10. They ___ fun in the yard. — have
11. Claire and Ava ___ counted to fifty. — have
12. Micah ___ Jin build a tower. — has
13. I have ___ Ava study. — seen
14. I ___ her study yesterday. — saw
15. I ___ Ava study her Bible every Sunday. — see
16. I have ___ breakfast already. — eaten
17. I ___ my last orange yesterday. — ate
18. I ___ eggs every day. — eat
19. I will ___ to church tonight. — go
20. I ___ to church last night. — went
21. I have ___ to church every night. — gone
22. Micah and Jin ___ next to each other. — sit
23. Claire ___ the Bible on the desk. — set

Lesson 32; Exercise 5; Day 160

1. lgnoa = along
2. grsua = sugar

Language Level 3 —Answer Keys

3. tlngee = gentle
4. gdee = edge
5. ngoe = gone
6. mgea = game
7. tgsea = stage
8. gnneei = engine
9. vgei = give
10. rmge = germ

Lesson 33; Exercise 2; Day 162

1. The pastor came for ___ visit. — an
2. He gave ___ cat a treat. — the
3. He ate ___ extra piece of pie. — a
4. I wore ___ coat. — those
5. Are ___ my shoes? — that
6. The cat lost ___ toy. — its
7. I'm sad ___ time to say goodbye. — it's
8. ___ jacket is this? — Who's
9. ___ coming for dinner? — Whose

Lesson 33; Exercise 3; Day 163

1. <u>Whale of a Story</u> is a fun book to read.
2. I was in a play called <u>The Story of Ruth</u>.
3. Have you watched <u>I Dig Dinosaurs</u> by Buddy Davis?

Lesson 33; Exercise 5; Day 165

1.
```
W W G B K N E E Z Q T E
D R N N V K P A C H E H
I O A V A T Z C A K T O
L N W S G W R E S T L E
N G D T T N B S T A R G
K N O C K L O G L S W N
T K M S W R O T E T P A
L A M B J M M X W L X T
B I T H U M B U Q E O T
```

Lesson 34; Exercise 1; Day 166

1. Student should name a pet.
2. Student should name a zoo animal.
3. Student should name a bird.
4. Student should name a color.

Lesson 34; Exercise 5; Day 170

1. fiddle or little
2. matter
3. current
4. full or tall
5. follow
6. tall or full
7. class
8. little or fiddle
9. dress
10. wiggle

Lesson 35; Exercise 1; Day 171

1. The little bird gave a tweet,
   And I thought that it sounded sweet.
2. I love to slowly walk that way.
   I wish I could be gone all day.
3. I love to drive along the coast.
   It is where I visit most.
4. When I drink a glass of milk,
   It goes down as smooth as silk.

Lesson 35; Exercise 2; Day 172

1. to — number
2. too — also or a lot
3. two — direction
4. there — belonging to others
5. their — they are
6. they're — a place
7. homophones — sound the same, different meanings
8. homonyms — same spelling, different meanings, different spelling

9. sour — tart
10. happy — glad
11. leave — go
12. jump — hop
13. arrive — come
14. leave — arrive
15. sad — glad
16. wet — dry
17. fast — slow
18. laugh — cry

Lesson 35; Exercise 3; Day 173
1. IN Why should we praise God?
2. D I like to sing at church.
3. E God is good!
4. IM Open your Bible to Genesis.
5. I will praise you, God.
6. We had salad, chicken, and fruit at the church picnic.
7. Micah, please read Psalm 67 to the class.
8. You, God, are worthy of praise.
9. Wow! God is good.
10. Oh, did you finish reading Psalm 67?
11. The girls ate their lunch.
12. Answers will vary
13. Mom said, "Be nice to each other."
14. does not = doesn't
15. we are = we're
16. I have = I've
17. Mister — Mr.
18. Miss — Ms.
19. Missus — Mrs.
20. Doctor — Dr.
21. Reverend — Rev.
22. Detective — Det.
23. Answers will vary.
24. Answers will vary.
25. Answers will vary.

Lesson 36; Exercise 2; Day 177
1. They gave the cat food.
2. photos
3. messes
4. tomatoes
5. city = cities
6. wolf = wolves
7. roof = roofs
8. dog's
9. cats'
10. The dog lost its toy.
11. It's under the couch.
12. Ava played with Claire's cat.
13. income
14. fast: faster fastest
15. tame: tamer tamest
16. Ava likes to ___ next to Claire. — sit
17. Claire ___ the Bible on the desk. — set
18. I wore ___ coat. — that
19. Are ___ my shoes? — those
20. ___ jacket is this? — Whose
21. ___ coming for dinner? — Who's
22. Answers will vary.
23. Answers will vary.

24. homophones
25. homonyms

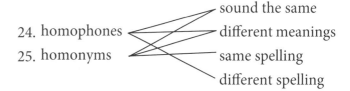
- sound the same
- different meanings
- same spelling
- different spelling

Language Lessons for a Living Education

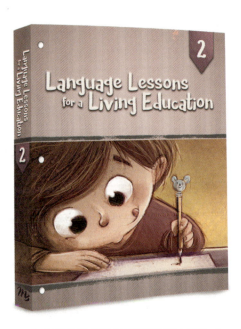

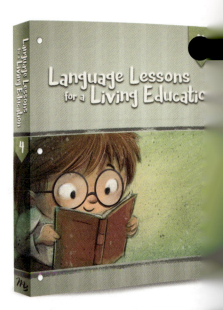

LANGUAGE LESSONS FOR A LIVING EDUCATION 2
GRADE 2

Incorporates picture study, memorization, grammar and punctuation, spelling & vocabulary, observation and application through creating their own stories through pictures and sentences, poems, psalms, and letters. Also develops early reading skills and gently develops narration skills.

9781683441229

LANGUAGE LESSONS FOR A LIVING EDUCATION 3
GRADE 3

Continuing with what the student has learned in Level 2, Book 3 will add to their reading, communication and observation skills. They will begin to write paragraphs. They will review and refine lessons from Level 2 in addition to learning new skills.

9781683441373

LANGUAGE LESSONS FOR A LIVING EDUCATION 4
GRADE 4

Will review previous grammar concepts and continue with what the student has learned in Level 3. Includes noun types, verb tenses, mechanics, and compositions.

9781683441380

VISIT MasterBooks.com — Where Faith Grows! — TO SEE OUR FULL LINE OF FAITH-BUILDING CURRICULUM OR CALL 800-999-3777

LEVELS 1-6
MATH LESSONS FOR A LIVING EDUCATION
A CHARLOTTE MASON FLAVOR TO MATH FOR TODAY'S STUDENT

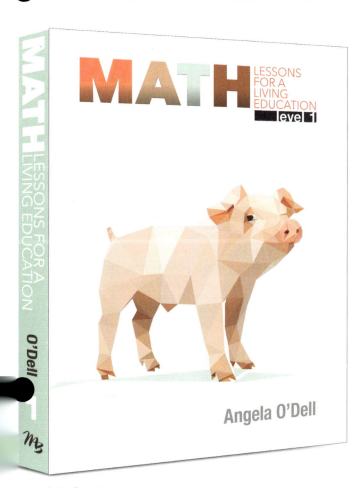

Level 1, Grade 1:
Learning numbers 0 to 100, circles and patterns, counting and addition, days of the week, and telling time.

Downloadable answer key
978-0-89051-923-3

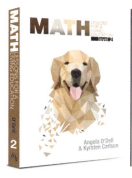

Level 2, Grade 2:
Subtraction, writing numbers to 100, introducing word problems and measurement, and dollars and cents.

Downloadable answer key
978-0-89051-924-0

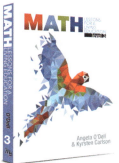

Level 3, Grade 3:
Column addition, introducing multiplication and division, and Roman numerals.

Removable answer key in back of book
978-0-89051-925-7

Level 4, Grade 4:
New fraction concepts, metric units of measurement, basic geometry, and averaging.

Removable solutions manual in back of book
978-0-89051-926-4

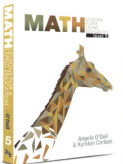

Level 5, Grade 5:
Factoring, improper fractions, common and uncommon denominators, and multiplying decimals.

Removable solutions manual in back of book
978-0-89051-927-1

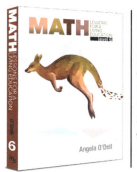

Level 6, Grade 6:
Real world math examples using advanced fractions, graphs, equations, and more!

Teacher Guide with solutions available
978-1-68344-024-6

Sample spreads from Book 1 — ATTRACTIVE FULL-COLOR LESSONS

MasterBooks CURRICULUM

AVAILABLE AT **MasterBooks.com** & OTHER PLACES WHERE FINE BOOKS ARE SOLD.

CHARLOTTE MASON INSPIRED
CURRICULUM THAT CONNECTS STUDENTS TO THEIR PAST... AND THEIR FUTURE!

Through this unique educational style, children develop comprehension through oral and written narration and create memories through notebooking and hands-on crafts. This is not just facts and figures - this is living history.

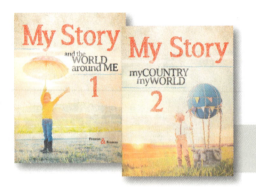

MY STORY 1-2 • Grades 1-2

An adventure-based curriculum that encourages families to explore the world together and understand it better from God's perspective. It is designed with elements that make weekly learning fun and interactive.

MY STORY Book 1: 978-1-68344-117-5
Book 2: 978-1-68344-118-2

AMERICA'S STORY 1-3 • Grades 3-6

America's Story brings American history alive through engaging storytelling, connecting students emotionally to the settings, characters, struggles, and victories experienced throughout American history.

AMERICA'S STORY
SET 1: 978-1-68344-057-4
Set 2: 978-1-68344-058-1
Set 3: 978-1-68344-059-8

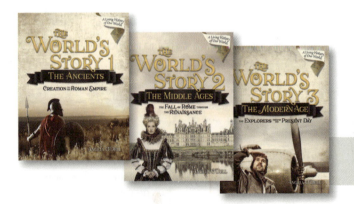

THE WORLD'S STORY 1-3 • Grades 6-8

Written from a strong Christian perspective, students will see God's hand throughout history and learn about how this history is still relevant to their lives today.

THE WORLD'S STORY
SET 1: 978-1-68344-135-9
Set 2: 978-1-68344-139-7
Set 3: 978-1-68344-140-3

VISIT MASTERBOOKS.COM — Where Faith Grows! — TO SEE OUR FULL LINE OF FAITH-BUILDING CURRICULUM OR CALL 800-999-3777.